D0481450

Oddly Normal

Oddly Normal

ONE FAMILY'S STRUGGLE

TO HELP THEIR TEENAGE SON

COME TO TERMS WITH HIS SEXUALITY

JOHN SCHWARTZ

GOTHAM BOOKS

GOTHAM BOOKS
Published by Penguin Group (USA) Inc.
375 Hudson Street, New York, New York 10014, U.S.A.
Penguin Group (Canada), 90 Eglinton Avenue East, Suite 700, Toronto, Ontario M4P 2Y3,
Canada (a division of Pearson Penguin Canada Inc.) · Penguin Books Ltd, 80 Strand, London
WC2R 0RL, England · Penguin Ireland, 25 St Stephen's Green, Dublin 2, Ireland (a division
of Penguin Books Ltd) · Penguin Group (Australia), 250 Camberwell Road, Camberwell,
Victoria 3124, Australia (a division of Pearson Australia Group Pty Ltd) · Penguin Books
India Pvt Ltd, 11 Community Centre, Panchsheel Park, New Delhi–110 017, India · Penguin
Group (NZ), 67 Apollo Drive, Rosedale, Auckland 0632, New Zealand (a division of
Pearson New Zealand Ltd) · Penguin Books (South Africa) (Pty) Ltd, 24 Sturdee Avenue,
Rosebank, Johannesburg 2196, South Africa

Penguin Books Ltd, Registered Offices: 80 Strand, London WC2R 0RL, England

Published by Gotham Books, a member of Penguin Group (USA) Inc.

First printing, November 2012
1   3   5   7   9   10   8   6   4   2

LIBRARY OF CONGRESS CATALOGING-IN-PUBLICATION DATA
Schwartz, John.
Oddly normal : one family's struggle to help their teenage son come to terms with his
sexuality / John Schwartz.—1st ed.
p.   cm.
ISBN 978-1-592-40728-6
1. Gay teenagers.   2. Parent and teenager.   3. Families.   I. Title.
HQ76.27.Y68S393   2012
306.76'60835—dc23   2012014369

Printed in the United States of America
Set in Sabon · *Designed by Elke Sigal*

While the author has made every effort to provide accurate telephone numbers, Internet
addresses, and other contact information at the time of publication, neither the publisher nor
the author assumes any responsibility for errors, or for changes that occur after publication.
Further, the publisher does not have any control over and does not assume any responsibility
for author or third-party websites or their content.

Penguin is committed to publishing works of quality and integrity.
In that spirit, we are proud to offer this book to our readers;
however, the story, the experiences, and the words
are the author's alone.

ALWAYS LEARNING   PEARSON

To the Lesbian, Gay, Bisexual
& Transgender Community Center
Youth Enrichment Services

and
Joseph

FOREWORD

Y ou have to come home," Jeanne said on the phone. Her voice was urgent, shaking. "Joe has taken a lot of pills."

Jeanne, my wife, had stepped into the house that late-spring afternoon to find our son Joseph stumbling around the bathroom in a daze. The room was scattered with pill bottles and bubble packs.

Joseph, then thirteen, is our youngest child, the last one still at home.

He had tried to take his own life.

We didn't know why he had done it; we didn't know whether the dozens of pills he had taken could cause a lethal overdose. We didn't know anything but our anguish.

Jeanne and I quickly talked out what needed to happen next. She had called the poison control center about the kinds of pills he had taken, and was told to get to a hospital right away. We decided not to wait for me to get home; she would drive Joseph to a nearby emergency room, taking the empty pill bottles with her. I would meet them there as soon as I could get across the Hudson River from my job in Manhattan.

In that instant, the story I had been struggling to finish—so important! The Second Amendment in the appellate courts!—meant nothing. I walked over to my editor to tell him about Joe. "Go," he said.

It's not easy to dash from New York City to New Jersey without a jetpack. Taxis were out. It wasn't the money that made me dismiss that option, though the trip would have cost more than my shoes. It was the beginning of the evening rush hour and the streets were jammed. I remembered the agony I had felt twenty-one years before, when I'd tried to cab over to Mount Sinai Hospital while Jeanne was giving birth to our first child. She had gone to the doctor's office for a routine appointment, the first one I'd missed. Of course, it turned out to be the big one: the doctor found a problem with the baby's heartbeat and decided to send Jeanne directly to the hospital. The doctor called to tell me to head over to Mount Sinai, adding in her calming voice that there was time to pick up our things from home. Once Jeanne got to the hospital, however, things had moved quickly, and the medical team scrambled to conduct an emergency caesarean section. Where was I during Jeanne's crisis? Stuck in traffic. It's the kind of experience that stays with you.

So: mass transit.

As my train rumbled out of Pennsylvania Station, under the Hudson River, and west across the Garden State, I thought about how much stress Joseph had been under lately, and how he had told me that he was occasionally seized with dark thoughts. He'd put it this way on a walk we had taken a few weeks before: "I am my subconscious's bitch." I'd asked if he wanted to see a therapist, but he'd said he didn't—that he'd be okay. Now, two weeks later, he was on his way to an emergency room.

What we didn't know was that Joseph had recently been dropping hints, gradually letting kids at school know that he is gay. And somehow, that day things had come to a head.

He had only let us in on his secret a week or two before, and it was welcome news. Frankly, we'd been waiting for what seemed like forever for him to work up the courage to tell us what we already knew. Coming out to us went well, but his second act, at school, had gone very badly. Then Joe had come home to an empty house. Jeanne, who works part-time as a crossing guard for our little suburban town, was working half a block away at the top of our street. Joe had gotten off the bus and passed her without a word; Jeanne saw that he looked upset but couldn't get home for another hour and a half. By then, he had gathered up the pills, stepped into the bathroom, and taken them, changing all of our lives.

This all happened a year before the nation would hear about a Rutgers University freshman named Tyler Clementi, who jumped to his death off the George Washington Bridge after his roommate secretly captured video of his encounter with another man. It was before most people were hearing about what was being called an epidemic of suicides by bullied gay teenagers. It was before the columnist and author Dan Savage kicked off a series of uplifting "It gets better" videos that encourage gay and lesbian kids to keep it together through their teen years, with a promise that life improves.

We didn't know enough about the research suggesting that LGBT youth are far more likely than straight kids to experience harassment, feel unsafe in academic settings, drop out of school, and more. It would be a year before a United States government report, "Healthy People 2010," would state that "gay male adolescents are two to three times more likely than their peers to attempt suicide."[1]

Back in 2009, all we knew was that we had one very unhappy son. After a couple of weeks in the hospital and then in the locked ward of a psychiatric treatment center, Joseph would come home to us. In the time since then, we've learned a lot about helping our boy become comfortable in his own skin; more important, Joe has learned a lot about it, too. The process has involved a lot of love, a lot of talking, and a few sessions with a hair colorist in the East Village.

Deciding to write about it all was not easy. A memoir is a tricky thing, full of potentially embarrassing moments and our own missed clues along the way, so agonizingly clear in hindsight. Embarrassment, however, seemed a risk worth taking if the story could possibly help others. Before I proposed the book, Joseph agreed that the story was worth telling.

A number of memoirs have come under fire in recent years; a journalistic cottage industry has grown up around debunking them. Many of the books have not held up to scrutiny. I decided, then, in taking on this book, to turn my reporter's toolkit on our own past in order to nail down the facts. I hold on to e-mail, and Jeanne and I supplement our conversations during the day with a steady stream of electronic correspondence that means our lives are dated and indexed in an electronic lifestream. I also take notes pretty much whenever I'm on the phone or in a meeting, and my telephone logs go back to 1994. I know it sounds compulsive, but it's proved invaluable in my work.

At Joseph's request, I have changed the names of his friends; I've also changed the names of some of the friends and neighbors I've interviewed who requested it.

This book includes discussions of the development of gay rights in the courts and in Congress, and some of the astonishing changes in popular culture that have helped move the country toward a greater acceptance of gay people. It also explores the work of social scientists on teen suicide and the pressures of growing up gay. These are topics I've reported on over the years. This time, I'm tying to weave the reporting threads together with our family's journey.

At the core, it's our story, about our gay child. If you are the parent of a gay child and you are reading this book, you will no doubt see that our gay child is not the same as your gay child. Joseph has some additional issues besides being gay that make him challenging in his own way. Your child might have other issues, other challenges. What our kids are likely to have in common is that they are both different.

Over the years, educators and psychologists tried to define Joe's troubles as medical and psychological issues. They offered a long series of diagnoses that we found confusing, conflicting, and more limiting than helpful. Sometimes, it seemed, the point of this medicalization was to describe a condition that might be treated with a pill. Other attempts at diagnosis seemed directed at taking him out of the educational mainstream and putting him on a side track that would leave him less likely to go to college. When we looked at Joe, we saw a kid with real promise.

He certainly had problems in school, problems with behavior, and problems in life. But to us, many of those troubles stemmed from something that, for years, no one else wanted to talk about: the increasingly clear fact that growing up gay in a straight world was causing him stress and pressure. The refusal to see being gay as a big part of the picture meant a lack of support for our son at critical times that could have made an enormous difference.

This story is told, then, from our perspective. A school administrator might tell a different story—Joseph was a difficult boy, and we surely made some of these folks miserable as well with our complaints and advocacy. We have reconstructed the past as thoroughly as we can, and I have gone back to interview many of the people involved. But it is still our story: what happened to our family, and how we dealt with it.

All this means that we don't claim to be presenting a step-by-step guide to raising a gay child. I couldn't imagine trying to write a self-help book; I've never felt that I was an expert in much of anything, and telling people how they should live their lives seems impossibly arrogant.

I agree with the journalist Timothy Noah about such works. In an amazing essay in *Slate*, the online magazine, he wrote, "Whenever I try to cope with one of life's predictable stress points by reading a self-help book, I can't manage it. My eyes glaze over. I think 'This person is an idiot,' or 'This person thinks I'm an idiot,' or 'Maybe I am an idiot, because I can't follow this.' Within minutes I toss the book aside and start digging around for a decent novel."[2]

Tim wrote that he takes greater meaning, and greater comfort, from memoirs. "What I've come to believe is that psychological advice isn't worth much if it isn't rooted in personal experience," he said. "So instead of reading self-help books I read memoirs about the kinds of experience I'm trying to cope with."

He wasn't looking for people just like him, he said—he was looking for a breadth of approaches. "It doesn't especially matter whether the author went about confronting his problem in a sensible way, nor even, necessarily, whether the author came out of the experience with a clear understanding of what he did right and what he did wrong. For instance, just about the last person I'd look to for personal advice about anything is Joan Didion. But when my wife died six years ago, I devoured Didion's best-selling memoir about widowhood, *The Year of Magical Thinking*, and other books about loss and grieving.

"Some of these books were more helpful than others, but all provided some form of 'self-help,' " he recalled. "Meanwhile, a stack of self-help books pressed on me by well-meaning friends gathered dust."

Tim's thoughts helped to guide me in writing this chimera of a book, which is part memoir, part journalistic exploration, and part mess. It's a book about raising a gay child in the age of Tyler Clementi, Proposition 8, and *Glee*. It's a book for parents about loving our children, especially when they do not yet know how to love themselves. It's a book about dealing with schools that still don't understand what to do with gay kids, and fighting for them with all your heart.

When one of our children is in distress, we'll do whatever we can do, go down any avenue, to ease that suffering. What our journey shows is that even the experts aren't always expert, and a huge part of parenting is learning to listen to your instincts.

You may have a gay child and be desperately unhappy about

that fact. You may have picked this book up thinking that it was going to help you figure out who to blame for your kid's turning out gay. You may even be looking for therapies to change the child's sexual orientation. This is not the book you are looking for, though it might be the book you need. Those issues will come up, but the point here is to show how important family love and support are, and how devastating the lack of them can be.

Jeanne and I are telling you about our bumpy ride in hopes that it will help other parents of gay kids—and maybe, parents of any kid who is different, who is mistreated by others, or who just may not accept himself—to know that they can find their own way to help a developing child handle the pain that can come from not fitting in. To help us all to relearn the most important parenting advice ever written, by Dr. Benjamin Spock: "Trust yourself. You know more than you think."

To let parents know that it gets better for them, too.

Besides, somebody's gotta pay for the hair dye.

CHAPTER ONE

Joseph Milton Schwartz came into the world just ahead of a blizzard. It was January 3, 1996, just days before much of the Washington area got hit by two feet of snow. The District of Columbia pretty much shuts down after the kind of light dusting that you might find in the bottom of a bag of Hostess Donettes, so this actual snowstorm paralyzed the Metro area for more than a week.

Joe was our third child, and labor progressed so uneventfully that at one point the obstetrician said, "Nothing much seems to be happening for a while—would you mind if I ran out and bought some tires?" He had heard about a place with nice prices.

While he was gone, Joe decided it was showtime. Jeanne's contractions grew more regular, the nurses wheeled her into the delivery room, and the returning doc got into position just in time to catch the little guy. Doctor Goodyear didn't even have a moment to put on all of his protective clothing, like the boo-ties. I noticed with quiet satisfaction that some of the gore spattered his very nice shoes.

We named Joe for my grandfather, who had passed away four years before, and who had started his life at the cusp of the twentieth century in Russia. The first Joe Schwartz made his way across the globe thanks to the professional ministrations of a yenta, who matched him and two other boys with three girls in Galveston, Texas. The girls' parents wanted good Yeshiva students from the old country for their daughters. The newlyweds-to-be met for the first time in Cuba, where the boys were sent to meet their brides; the boys made their marital choices at the gangplank.

Grandpa Joe, now married to an American and able to enter the United States legally, took his part in the American story: he started out sweeping the floors in a clothing store on Market Street until he learned English, then moved across the street to a competing store. When the first store failed, he was able to buy the building. He called it Schwartz's, selling pants in seven languages but never losing his slight Russian accent. A small man with big blue eyes and an engaging manner, he was loved in my hometown. I hoped that giving our Joseph his name might bestow a little of Grandpa's menschy character and sense of adventure. And when I brought baby Joseph back to Galveston for a family wedding and introduced him as Joe Schwartz, some of the older friends had tears in their eyes.

In any case, a boy named for a Russian immigrant should be able to deal with a little snow. We got Joseph home a day before the storm. In the snow-blanketed quiet of Takoma Park,

Maryland, over the next couple of weeks, our newly enlarged family of five lived on lasagna brought by neighbors and settled in for our reintroduction to the world of diapers, baby bottles, and sleeplessness.

We had been moving around the country as I went from job to job. Jeanne and I had come to New York in 1985 after college, when I'd been hired at *Newsweek*, and so our daughter, Elizabeth, and son Sam were New Yorkers; then in 1993 the *Washington Post* offered me a job writing about science and technology. So we headed south to a sweet bungalow in Takoma Park, a common landing strip for writers like me. That's where we were when Joseph came along.

Jeanne and I were feeling pretty good about ourselves as parents by that point—semipro at least. The two older kids had introduced us to what seemed like the entire list of childhood diseases and conditions, accidents and developmental milestones, and we had survived each one.

Elizabeth and then Sam had given us a great study in contrasts. Elizabeth behaved as if she had read the same early child development books that we were reading, and hit every milestone precisely when it was supposed to happen. She took her first steps on her first birthday, waiting and testing her legs until she could walk with confidence.

We were careful, fretful readers of the child-rearing books, which were filled with such helpful and often conflicting advice. They all seemed to deliver one message: "You're doing it wrong." The one point we did take away from many of them was to avoid pushing gender stereotypes; don't force dolls on girls. She's not going to become an engineer or governor if you've filled her head with influences like Barbie saying "Math is hard!" So we jammed our apartment with dolls *and* toy trucks, girly dresses *and* building blocks. The fact that she preferred the dolls, and loved the pink tutu she wore to ballet, were signposts of her own emerging personality.

Sam, born three years later, was all boy. He seemed to have come into the world with fully developed leg muscles, and had an odd kind of density to him that you felt when you tried— *oof!*—to pick him up. As soon as he could crawl, he got over to Elizabeth's pile of toys and methodically pulled out every truck. *The Y chromosome is strong with this one*, I thought, and told friends, "He's got a lot of yang."

It was apparent in everything. Sam didn't walk; from the start, he ran. He'd stand up, pitch his big head forward, and with gravity pulling him, he'd stumble ahead at top speed. How did he stop? By slamming into things. Sofas. Walls. Parents. He didn't care. He was a running hugger, hitting with enough force to nearly knock us over. It wasn't long before he earned the nickname "Saminator."

Just as Elizabeth had scared us with the emergency delivery at the hospital, Sam had a worrying medical issue of his own: a concavity at his sternum that seemed to contribute to labored breathing. He almost sounded as if he was snoring, and audibly enough that a little girl at one of Elizabeth's ballet recitals shouted out amid the quiet, "There's a *pig* in here!" The grunting was so loud that a friend we encountered one afternoon on Broadway on the noisy Upper West Side stopped in midsentence, tilting his head and asking, "Is that *him*?" The doctor prolonged the time that he recommended Sam stay with us at night, warning us that he might develop apnea; a babysitter refused to take him, telling us bluntly that she thought he would die. We could hardly sleep at night, listening for the soft grunting to suddenly stop, and terrified that we might lose him.

I would think about those panicked nights years later, when I'd watch our fearless Sam on the high school football field. And on the lacrosse field. And on the wrestling mat.

With Joey, then, we were prepared for the next crisis. Instead, we got the most amazing thing: an easy baby. He worked through the timetable of child development as Elizabeth had, as if he was working through a punch list. He was ahead of time on one thing: Joey was early to smile, and to laugh—especially if you planted a loud, tickling raspberry on his belly. He was a fat, happy baby, presenting a sly grin to the world as if telling you that he was in on the joke.

Piece of cake, Jeanne thought.

Growing into toddlerhood, he was much easier to pick up than his solid older brother, as if his bones were hollow. He'd wrap his arms and legs around Jeanne for a clinging, joyous hug as she carried him around; she called him her "spider monkey."

Like his sister and brother, Joe was a language sponge, soaking up words at an amazing clip and becoming weirdly articulate. That's not so surprising: I earn my living by talking, listening, and typing. Jeanne studied to be an archivist, and read book after book aloud to each child. She began with *Pat the Bunny* and *Busy, Busy Toddlers* ("I am busy all the time!"). Then they would graduate to tougher fare, including the entire *Lord of the Rings* trilogy. Jeanne read every page to each child in turn.

Each child's approach to the stories was a window into a developing self. Jeanne read them *The Runaway Bunny*, the classic children's story by Margaret Wise Brown, who was also the author of *Goodnight Moon*. In case you missed *The Runaway Bunny*, it is about a little rabbit who tells his mother, "I am running away."[3]

The mother responds that if he runs away, "I will run after you. For you are my little bunny." He then describes the fanciful escapes he will make, and she answers each one. When he says he will become a fish in a trout stream, she responds, "I will become a fisherman and I will fish for you." He talks about becoming a crocus in a hidden garden, a sailboat, a circus performer on a flying trapeze. Always, the mother says, she will go to him, find him, hug him, and bring him home.

Elizabeth was lulled by the musical language and the sweetness of the illustrations. Three years later, though, Sam reacted to the book with anger and youthful scorn. Why can't she just let him have fun? He wanted to know. What is wrong with that mother?

Jeanne came to agree, thinking, "Yeah, there is something wrong with that mother bunny—so needy! No wonder he keeps running away. . . ."

She thought about giving the book to the library sale but held off. Then came Joe, who listened to the words with wide-eyed pleasure. No matter what you do, he seemed to hear, your mother will love you. No matter how far you wander, you can always come home. She wasn't smothering him. She was accepting him.

The kids didn't just pick up language, but also accent and attitude. Elizabeth acquired language skills in our upper Manhattan neighborhood and in a preschool next to Central Park; by the age of three was asking for "Devil Doawgs" and asking guests if they would like some "cawfee." She also had an endearingly odd way with language: at four years old, she held up a freshly washed grape to one of our friends during a party and asked, "Would you like a wet grape in your life?" Sam was a more straightforward talker but employed turns of phrase that could take my breath away. Sam and I once had a fight on a trip to the Catskills when he was nine or ten. When we apologized to each other, Sam said to me, "I love you more than a diamond."

Joe had all that and more. His babysitter hailed from Grenada, and little Joey developed an accent that was semi-British with an island lilt. When we enrolled him in preschool in Takoma Park, the teachers asked what country we'd adopted him from.

That sly smile, once language came along, got a sassy tongue to go with it. When Jeanne and I visited the preschool one morning, we approached the children's bathroom, which was a hallway enclosure with a privacy curtain at the front. A little girl was pulling up her dress to hop on the pot, and had forgotten to close the curtain. Joey called out as he passed, "I don't need to see your undopants!"

He was, in other words, our son.

Jeanne and I built our word-drunk relationship on language and laughs from the start. We met in 1975, both of us just eighteen. Classes at the University of Texas were about to begin, and we were moving into Beauford H. Jester dormitory, a behemoth that housed thousands.

"Jeanne! This is the guy I was telling you about!" It was Mike Godwin, a Houston kid I'd met that summer at orientation. He called me over to meet his girlfriend. Mike and I had hit it off instantly at orientation, finding that we both knew the words to practically every song by Tom Lehrer, and had the courage, or temerity, to sing them. We had also, as it turned out, similar taste in movies and books.

And girls. A freckled redhead, Jeanne pushed just about every button I've got. And she was wearing less clothing than anyone I'd ever seen who wasn't at the beach.

Looking cool in the blast-furnace heat of an Austin August, she wore short shorts and a lightweight T-shirt that was held up with spaghetti straps and luck. There was a unicorn on the front of it, and the fabric was distractingly thin. *This*, I thought, *is interesting.*

And the attraction went beyond first impressions. When we talked, it wasn't this careful boy-girl game of saying nothing in a friendly, flirty way. She *talked*, honestly, profanely, hilariously. The books she loved. The movies she loved. The *comic books* she loved! She owned every Howard the Duck! Later, I would know the word for what I was experiencing: nerdgasm.

When Jeanne was excited about telling me something, she would bounce on the balls of her feet and slap my chest with both hands, *patta-patta-patta pat*! Her eyes glowed. She was just plain fun.

She and Mike were breaking up, she said, though it was unclear whether she had let him know that. Before the middle of that first semester, we were dating. Mike would go on to become a pioneering civil liberties lawyer of the online world and earn a kind of Net immortality as the creator of Godwin's Law. That's the humorous meme that states the longer an online discussion goes on, the likelihood that someone will criticize a point by bringing up a comparison to Nazis approaches 100 percent.

Mike got fame, and I got the girl. Jeanne and I rented our first place together, and talked about getting married, made plans, let it slide; stayed together, saw other people, became closer—and, after nearly nine years together, we made it official in 1984 with a sweet, raucous wedding in Austin. A year later, we were heading to New York City to start my journalism career.

And so here we were, twelve years later and three kids richer. By the time Joseph showed up, we had stopped worrying about maintaining a gender-neutral play environment and other theories we had incorporated with Elizabeth and Sam. With a third child, you're lucky to remember to change the diapers. But the piles of toys were still around.

Just after Joseph was born, Sam growled, "I won't share my toys with him." No problem! Joe went for the dolls. He and Jeanne would sit on the floor, dressing up the plastic figures and trying different combinations. As Jeanne recalled it, "Barbie never looked so fabulous. He would layer her clothing, carefully coordinating her outfits just so."

Joe dressed himself with just as much care, pleading for light-up shoes with pink accents and rhinestones. We hesitated; would people give us trouble about putting our toddler in pink light-up shoes? The salesman, clearly gay, smiled and said, "If more parents would buy boys pink shoes when they asked for them, the world would be a better place." That clinched the sale.

Our attempts to get Joey into sports, which Sam had loved so much, were frustrating bordering on the disastrous. The first day of soccer practice, the coach took his group of five-year-olds out onto the grass to learn the fundamentals of the game and run them up and down the field. Joe lay down on the sidelines and refused to get up, like a protester gone limp in the face of the cops. The coaches curtly asked me to take him home; they needed to focus their attention on the kids who wanted to play. I realized we might have to find other, less physical activities for Joe.

Were these signs? It's easy to connect dots in hindsight. But plenty of boys play with dolls, though they tend to be "action figures" that fight instead of accessorize.

All we knew in those early years was that we had ourselves a fairly girly boy. And that was fine with us. I never was very much in the machismo department, having always been the last kid picked at school for any sport. Sam, even as a little kid, brimmed with enough manliness for the whole family.

My mother, at least, picked up the clues quickly in Joe's interests and enthusiasms. Galveston had a thriving gay community, and Mom loved her gay friends dearly. On one visit, when Joseph was offered two shirts, he eagerly grabbed the pink one. She looked at me and slowly lifted her eyebrows. And smiled.

Of course, none of this proved anything. We knew plenty of little boys with a flamboyant streak, including Sam. One Halloween, third-grader Sammy said he wanted to wear a ball gown as his costume. With his broad shoulders, our burly boy looked hilarious in the ersatz satin and played it for laughs: future nose guard in a dress. The kid had panache.

The next year, Joseph, age three, asked if he could be a "disco yady" for Halloween. The request was different. This was no joke. In fact, he said it with a kind of yearning.

None of it had to mean anything. Sam had gotten so much

attention for being the belle of the ball the year before, and what kid wouldn't want to enjoy the spotlight?

Still, we began to wonder, what with Joseph's regular raids on Elizabeth's jewelry boxes for shiny baubles, and his desire to use them to decorate one of Sam's cast-off plastic castles. The castle had been made for battling action figures, but Joseph was draping beads and treasures on it, making it all, as he'd say, "prettiful."

Was our preschooler gay?

CHAPTER TWO

Whter do you know? When might you first be able to tell that your child is gay?

We felt we were seeing signals very early in Joseph's life; come on—how big a hint is wanting to look like a "disco yady"? But then, couldn't it just be a phase? Our family has always felt like a sitcom, and this was the sitcom way: wackiness ensues, and things are wrapped up by the hour's end.

Many parents would be upset by the thought that one of their children could turn out to be gay. But we didn't see it that way; it seemed obvious to us that sexuality is biological in origin, as baked into who you are as eye color and height.

When it comes to things that we can change and believe that we should, we're on it. There are attributes that any parent would want to fix or improve as a child develops. If any of our children were starting to look like bullies, we would nudge them in a kinder direction. If any of them seemed seriously disturbed, we would rush them into therapy. But we'd no more try to change a child's sexual orientation than his biological tendency to write with his left hand instead of his right.

And it's not as if we're somehow special for thinking that: the realization that biology, far more than environmental factors, shapes sexual orientation has been growing as the scientific proof piles up.

A 2011 Gallup survey showed that 40 percent of Americans say that being gay or lesbian is "something a person is born with."[4] The percentage of people who believed that sexual orientation is a product of the environment is slightly higher—42 percent—but within the four-point margin of error in the survey. What's interesting about the number is the trend: in 1978, just 13 percent of people said that biology is the basis of sexuality, and 56 percent said it was environment. The side that says "it's nature, not nurture" has been growing steadily.

Jeanne and I had grown up with gay friends and relatives. Jeanne's cousin Jim, who we visited at the East Texas college where he taught theater and then worked around the world for the U.S.O., showed us you could be gay just about anywhere. My seventh-grade math teacher came out and bought Galveston's storied gay bar, the Kon Tiki.

Jeanne and I had seen plenty of anti-gay prejudice, too—it was as common to hear the shouted calls of "Faggot!" in our west campus neighborhood in Austin as "Hook 'em!" We knew that kind of hatred had no place in our home or our lives.

So with Joe, we simply wanted to know—as any parent does—who our child is. We hoped to see the future in the tea leaves of his early behavior.

Our feeling that Joe might be gay got stronger over time as

the clues piled up, and well before even Joseph quite knew what was going on himself.

Not every gay person knows from the start, and it's not as if everyone who is going to be gay or straight or bisexual is issued a membership card at birth. One of my best friends at the newspaper who is gay told me that he dated women until he was twenty-five.

The friend, Rich Meislin, told me this during a conversation about whether Joseph might be gay. Like other friends who we talked to about this when Joe was little, both gay and straight, he skeptically suggested that it was awfully early to tell. I agreed that there was no need to jump the gun.

A few weeks later, Rich met Joseph Schwartz, age six, at a *New York Times* staff picnic. We sat together at a long picnic table, and Joseph explained to Rich that he would someday live in a house on a tropical island, decorated in bright island colors and green growing things inside and out. As Joe went on in great detail about the decor, the amusement on Rich's face became a kind of a glow. Later, Rich pulled me aside and asked, "*How old* is he?" as if my son had just set some youth division record for triggering his gaydar.

Many people do seem to come into the world more like Joe did, with their sexual identity in place from the get-go. John Waters, the director of outrageous movies like *Pink Flamingos* and the original *Hairspray*, recorded a video for National Coming Out Day in 2011 with a funny riff on the fact that "coming out, it just seems sort of *square* to me," though he knew it was important to many people. "I always knew I was gay," he said. "I knew I was gay the moment I saw Elvis Presley when I was probably ten years old. I thought, 'what the hell is *that*?'"[5]

In that way, at least, John Waters appears to be normal: Researchers Eric M. Dubé and Ritch C. Savin-Williams determined from a 1999 study of 139 gay youngsters that the average age they became aware of their sexual orientation was ten.[6] Another study by Anthony R. D'Augelli and colleagues put the average age for awareness of same-sex attraction among boys at twelve, and among girls at fourteen.[7]

Hank Stuever of the *Washington Post* described a kind of moment of truth for even younger kids in a brilliant essay about Wonder Woman and the gay boys who idolized her as children. "Long before these certain little boys know or realize what being homosexual even is, they will often fixate on some strong or larger-than-life female idol, and she won't let go. The diva inside unfurls. It could be triggered by a movie goddess, a pop singer, a chick on a scooter escaping secret agents. It could be as unlikely as a *Life* magazine spread of Pat Nixon showing off the White House."[8]

"The diva inside unfurls." For Stuever, the passage was autobiographical; he is gay, and in a 2002 interview with *Metro Weekly*, a gay magazine in Washington, D.C., he said that although many people realize only in adolescence or adulthood that they are gay, he didn't identify with their "coming-out stories." It seemed odd to him, he said, that "this day you weren't gay, and then there was this day that you were."

His experience, and, he suggested, the experiences of many other people's, was less dramatic and more flamboyant: "extremely fabulous five-year-olds who swished around the house and made it very clear what we were, whether anybody was able to read that text or not. I was a fabulous five-year-old and my mother knew it."[9]

How fabulous? As he recalled in the interview, "My dad pulled up in the driveway one day and I was out in the front yard dressed as Wonder Woman. I had tied up three neighborhood kids to our little suburban tree. I had on my sister's tube top, knee-high red socks, and aluminum foil wrapped around my wrists."

Wonder Woman was what scientific experts refer to as a Big Honking Clue. Now, clues aren't everything: a number of studies suggest that about a third of gay men recall having masculine childhoods. And while some studies suggest the vast majority of effeminate boys grow up to be gay, some put the percentage closer to about half, which would mean that half of effeminate boys grow up to be straight.

Science isn't great at explaining the "why" of behavior—that is, why some gay children might clomp around in his mother's high heels, or act more like a girl than a boy. Instead, studies give us the correlations between, say, effeminate behavior in childhood and adult sexual orientation. And those studies are telling.

An enormous body of research supports the idea that sexual orientation can make itself known in surprisingly little kids, even as early as three years old. The Kinsey Institute found in 1981 that "gender nonconformity greatly increases the likelihood of that child's becoming homosexual regardless of his or her family background and regardless of how much the child identifies with either parent." The researchers were also careful to state, however, that "gender nonconformity does not inevitably signal future homosexuality."

The most famous research comes from Richard Green, a longtime scholar of human sexuality. His landmark study is named *The Sissy Boy Syndrome: The Development of Homosexuality.*

Really, it is.

Published in 1987, the fifteen-year study tracked the lives of forty-four boys who were extremely effeminate and thirty-four who were "gender conforming." Green found that fully thirty of the thirty-four girly boys would later prove to be homosexual or bisexual adults, while only one of the more masculine group of thirty-four turned out to be gay. (In girls, other studies suggest, the rate of gender nonconforming growing up to be gay is much lower, at about 25 percent.)

The sample size is small, of course, and the group was made up of boys who were so effeminate that parents were concerned about their behavior and brought them into counseling; the results are not as pronounced in the broader population.

But the underlying finding of the study was clear: your fabulous five-year-old is likely to be a gay adult. Not because effeminate behavior causes homosexuality, but because it is a semaphore signal from within of what's likely to fully emerge later in life. Green also found that most of his very effeminate boys became more masculine as they grew up, butching up to conform to social norms.

Green's work has been used by those who are uncomfortable with homosexuality to suggest the opposite: that tolerating sissy behavior can cause someone to become gay. I contacted Green, who stressed in an e-mail that those folks have got him wrong. "I never argued that being a feminine boy made a boy a homosexual man. While he may socialize more comfortably with girls, most of whom will evolve attraction to males, this will not make him homosexual. My educated guess is that cross-gender behavior in boys is the age-appropriate expression of underlying homosexuality."

Green's early work has been repeated, with similar results. By 1995, researchers J. Michael Bailey and Kenneth J. Zucker would write that their review of research in the field suggested a lower percentage than Green had found: 51 percent of "boys with the requisite degree of cross-sex-typed behavior" will become homosexual. They added the point made in much of the analysis of Green's study: "boys referred to clinics for cross-sex-typed behavior are more extreme in that respect" than typical boys. Overall, they concluded, "Homosexual individuals recall substantially more childhood cross-sex-typed behavior than do heterosexuals of the same sex." Studies that rely on people's memories of childhood can be biased by our tendency to reshape our past into neat stories that explain our present selves, but which may not be accurate. In this study, however, the authors noted that studies following children over time supported their memory-based findings for men. As for tomboys, they admitted, "analogous studies for women remain to be done."[10]

All this research tells us little about any individual child, of course, leaving parents of a fabulous five-year-old guessing what's really going on with their kid and wondering if their intuition is correct. There's an app for that: a French company briefly offered an application in 2011 for Android phones named "Is my son gay?"[11] The onscreen image of a somber, pensive mother suggests that the creators of the program believe they are selling to a crowd that will dread the answer. The website for the product says that the program asks "20 questions to know more about your son," after which "you'll have the proven answer to a question you might have since maybe a long time." And all for just $2.69!

I'm an iPhone guy, so I couldn't test the product myself, and within a month after its controversial entrance into the market, it was gone. According to an account on MSNBC's Gadgetbox website, some of the questions included:

- Does he take a long time to do his hair?
- Does he read the sports page in the newspaper?
- Does he have a complicated relationship with his father?
- Are you divorced?
- During his childhood, was he timid or discreet?
- Does he like musical comedies?
- Is he a fan of divas (Madonna, Britney Spears)?

Somehow, I think a parent's intuition has got to offer a little more insight than that, and even $2.69 seems like overcharging. But it does prove one thing: for every fear, there's someone willing to exploit it, and, potentially, a market as well. Parents have plenty of fears. When we were new to the game of having children, a parent of another newly expanded family joked that the perfect magazine for all of us would be *Fret: The Magazine of Anxious Parenting.*

There is another question here, one that unsettles many parents, about whether these same signals suggest a child will become transgendered—that is, a woman who believes she is a man trapped in a female body, and vice versa, and may want sexual reassignment surgery later in life. There's no conclusive research on this, and the debates over whether or not to start a child down the road to such surgery, and when, could fill a book of their own. In fact, they have filled many books already. For now, let's just hear what Alice Dreger, a bioethicist at Northwestern University, has to say on the state of the science when it comes to early behavior suggesting that a child will be gay or transgendered. As she put it in the Hastings Center Report in 2009, "gender-atypical young children are far more likely to end up homosexual than gender-typical young children, and they appear to be much more likely to end up non-transgender gay men or lesbian women than transgender men or women."[12]

In other words, that fabulous five-year-old is far more likely to end up gay than transgendered.

CHAPTER THREE

As Joseph turned out to be a different kind of boy, we rolled with it—initially surprised, and occasionally amused.

He was four by the time we moved back to the Northeast. An editor for the *New York Times* had called. He liked my stuff and wondered if I'd be interested in making a move. It wasn't a hard choice: if they wanted me, I wanted them. After an epic job interview process, Jeanne and I found ourselves deciding to move to the New York area in a matter of weeks, scouting houses on a whirlwind tour of northern New Jersey.

We focused on a town that fit right in the overlapping middle of a mental Venn diagram of our lives with three circles: cost, schools, and commute. Homes there were more affordable than those in Montclair, which is a white-hot market for families decamping from the Upper West Side of Manhattan. The commute was dead easy: a train that stopped in town gets to Midtown a half hour later on most days. And the schools were so well regarded that Jay Mathews, a great education reporter at the *Washington Post*, had ranked the high school number one in the nation in his book *Class Struggle: What's Wrong (and Right) with America's Best Public High Schools*. The book, of course, was casually left on several dining room tables in the houses we looked at, as if the owners had just been rereading their favorite passages before having been called away.

Most of the homes we toured were priced out of the range of a single-income family whose breadwinner doesn't run a hedge fund. I asked the Realtor for the stack of multiple listing service printouts and ordered them from the cheapest to most expensive. And the page for the cheapest one pleaded, "Not a drive-by!"

Clearly, most people had driven by. In a market so hot that bidding wars turned into fistfights, this unlovely home had sat on the market for five months. It was on a busy street. It was built on so many split levels that the stairs had a kind of M. C. Escher weirdness. And the owner had painted it pink. Really, really pink. The neighborhood kids called it the "Barbie house."

But it also had four bedrooms and two bathrooms.

We took it. And painted it blue. Our new neighbors thanked us for that, and of course the neighborhood kids started calling it the "Ken house." And the big empty house became a big crowded home, filled with a family of five and toys and computers and the smells of food.

Elizabeth and Sam settled into their new neighborhood and schools. They soon discovered that this was a fancier suburb than the one we had left behind in Maryland. When one of Sam's new friends came by the house, he exclaimed, "Your whole house could fit inside of my house, with some room left over!" Our kids knew that we didn't have the kind of wealth that the people in town showed off. Instead, we told them we were neither rich nor poor, saying, "We have enough money."

For that first year, Joe, still a year away from kindergarten, stayed home with Jeanne. They played and visited the tiny local zoo and spent a lot of quality time dressing Barbie.

When the next fall came around, Joseph was excited to be heading off to kindergarten.

We weren't worried. If there actually had been a magazine named *Fret*, our subscription would have lapsed after seeing how well the schools dealt with our older kids. We figured in these modern times, with rising tolerance for gay people, the schools would know what to do with an effeminate kid who might be gay. Right?

We would find out soon enough that while it's okay for millionaire entertainers to be gay, girly little grade schoolers still have some problems.

Joe had begun reading the year before, and was plowing through the Harry Potter books and a series of British books for kids, Scholastic's Horrible Histories and Horrible Science, that made their subjects fun. So this was the kid who could tell you all about Archimedes' death ray, the sun-focusing mirror that the Greek scientist is said to have created 2,200 years ago to defend his land from ship attack.

Joe's intense reading habits were no surprise to either of us. As soon as I had become a confident reader, I attacked the family's *World Book Encyclopedia*, determined to read every article. I didn't make it all the way through, but I made a substantial dent, which laid the foundation for later triumphs in trivia games. Jeanne was the kid who read *Don Quixote* in elementary school and pulled down works of philosophy from her father's bookshelf. Elizabeth had been a devoted reader, too, and while it took Sam longer to get interested in the written word, he would later prove to be formidable.

We didn't know how Joe's kindergarten teacher would react to our tiny autodidact. To our relief, she was tickled by the bright kid who wanted to answer every question and had a startling vocabulary.

One day in class she asked the kids to say a word beginning with the letter *U*. Joseph's hand shot up and he said, "Ungulate."

When she told us the story, the teacher laughed and said, "I had to look it up!"

It was a happy year, though Joseph became more emotional and broody for a time that spring. On one of Jeanne's volunteer visits to the classroom to serve pizza, the teacher asked if there was anything wrong at home. Jeanne explained that I was out of town. In early 2002, I was spending weeks at a time on the road for work: the Enron scandal had blown open in Houston. The editor of the paper at the time would proudly talk about "flooding the zone" on big stories, and I was part of the flood. Jeanne, meanwhile, was juggling three kids who attended an elementary school, a middle school, and a high school. And, any reporter will tell you, when we are on long reporting trips, cars and major appliances choose to break down. In other words, yes, there was a bit of stress at home, now that you mention it.

It was our first sign that Joseph was sensitive to the ambient level of stress around him. It wasn't a big problem for this teacher, though—when he was upset, she let him sit in the corner and read.

He adored her. For one class project, the kids had made large images of themselves on stiff paper and cut them out, then colored and decorated them with glitter and spangles. Joe's artwork was always pretty heavy on the glitter. And the self-image he created was blinding, glorious, open-armed, and smiling. The teacher gave him a treasure: the image she had made of herself. He brought both home with him, and Jeanne put them up together: Joseph and his teacher, shining and happy.

Joe got along well with all the kids, but Jeanne noticed he was far more attuned to the girls than with the boys. He'd come home from school and his chatter was, "Elena says this. Alison says that." He was fascinated with how they talked among themselves and how they played. Jeanne got the impression from the conversations that the class was heavily unbalanced, with far more girls than boys. She checked the class directory and saw to her surprise that the class was evenly divided.

There was one boy Joseph enjoyed talking about at home. He was tall, smart, and well liked, a beautiful child who had shown up in the middle of the school year. He and Joseph had found plenty to talk about at first, but by the end of kindergarten they had a running conflict. The boy complained that Joseph stood too close to him, and those small beginnings turned to harsh words; the two children became schoolyard enemies. Jeanne couldn't help but wonder if Joseph hadn't been attracted to the boy, and whether we were getting a first taste of what things would be like as Joseph unconsciously acted on attraction and rejection.

Jeanne had taken one precaution before the school year began. "I had quietly put all of the Barbies and their magnificent clothing away." She worried that Joe would insist on taking his fashionable dolls to school for show and tell, and "I didn't even want him talking to the other kids about Barbie and her fabulous wardrobe."

This wasn't based on research into the growing shelves of studies of gender identity—the experts conflict, anyway. It was based instead on Jeanne's intuition. "I don't know if it was right or wrong to edit his personality so early in the game," she says.

I agreed that the Barbies should go, though. We both knew that even kindergarten could be a tough room, and that early labels stick. "I didn't want him starting out on the wrong foot," Jeanne says, "making a mistake in kindergarten in a school where you were in the same building with the same children for six long years."

Joseph wondered where his favorite things had gone, and Jeanne felt strong pangs of regret. But she left the other prettiful things in his room, including that plastic castle, ornamented with every shiny thing Joseph could find: the beads, the costume jewelry filched from Elizabeth's trove, and the pewter wizards, their upheld wands topped with crystal globes.

"His room was still gay enough," Jeanne says, "if that was what he needed."

We had built his first closet.

We ended the year of kindergarten thinking that our younger boy was on a good path. The next few years would prove how wrong we were.

Joe's problems in the classroom would begin to outnumber his successes, and it weighed on him. At a time when we needed better lines of communication with the school to discuss the troubles he faced, the school went through a change. The businesslike but welcoming principal who had been in charge when we first arrived in town resigned. Parents could go to her to discuss whatever might be going on in the classroom. When we had problems at the school, they were quickly resolved, with no fuss. To us, her policy was something many schools talk about but not enough of them achieve: child-centered learning.

She was replaced when Joe entered first grade by a principal who prided himself on his management skills, but who seemed to define management as keeping the teachers happy. It wasn't hard to see why: in a town with more than its share of high-strung professionals, the parents can be pretty tough. Another elementary school principal in town told the story of a pregnant mother who stopped by his office after touring the school with her two small children in tow. "I have *three* exceptional children," the mother snapped, "What are you going to do for them?"

Our new principal placed himself as a buffer between those hard-nosed characters and his faculty. Parents are with you for a few years; many teachers have tenure. So he greeted the parents sunnily each day at the car drop-off line, opening the doors even in winter. But once inside the school, there was a colder feel: if there was a conflict with a teacher, the parents were nearly always wrong. For the kids, visits to his office became empty rituals, with the kid getting what Joseph came to call "lecture number 259" instead of encountering any real effort to find out what was going on. For the parents, it was like talking to an empty chair.

Meanwhile, Joseph was beginning to feel isolated at school. He had always been different, of course—that vocabulary of his would amuse and fascinate grown-ups, but he tended to baffle the other kids, who nicknamed him "Webster," for the dictionary. He preferred talking with adults. As a day camp counselor told us, "He tells jokes, and they don't get them. We get them, but they don't."

Now gender roles were coming into the mix in a big way as well. Boys were becoming more boyish. In those early grades, many of them already knew the full starting lineup of the Jets, which had far more relevance to their lives than ungulates and Archimedes. Joseph, even without a Barbie at show-and-tell, was fitting in less and less. And conformity is important in elementary school.

Normal little boys also like to play sports. Not this little boy. Joe's bad experience with Pee Wee soccer reminded me of my own misery as a small, unathletic kid growing up in Texas. Always the last picked and the most picked on, I grew up with no interest in sports. I don't even watch games on television, so Joseph wasn't going to learn about the Jets or the Yankees from me.

By comparison, the Saminator's emerging prowess in multiple sports was a point of pride and wonder—around the age of ten, he'd developed a wicked slide tackle. Sam's dresser became a platform for his many sports trophies. Joseph's would eventually display trophies and medals for his abilities on the piano and in singing. But that wouldn't help him fit in with the boys.

The girls were starting to wall Joseph off, too. As they grew into second and third graders, many of the girls were starting to see boys as yucky. A boy who wanted to talk with them was even worse. They preferred spending time with one another and were too conscious of their emerging roles to be seen hanging out with boys at school.

Socializing outside of school only seemed to deepen the

differences. Playdates with the boys in the neighborhood fell flat. They wanted to ride bikes and throw a ball around. Joseph wanted to play computer games. Knowing that he had a closer affinity with the girls than the boys, we'd set up some playdates with girls and hoped they would go better. He had a great time on a handful of visits. It was going well, until he got to school after a couple of get-togethers, and some kids chanted, "Joseph and Elena sitting in a tree K-I-S-S-I-N-G." Joseph and the girl were horrified. The playdates stopped.

The subject was *u*-sounds.

Jeanne had been asked to come in for a meeting with Joe's first-grade teacher. The teacher had complaints. Concerns. Among them: she had given the children an in-class assignment asking to use a sentence with a word or words containing the "short-*u*" sound.

Joe had written, "Pick up the fucking gunk."

This was inappropriate, she told Jeanne. But when Jeanne told me about it later, the writer in me couldn't help but be a little proud.

"Three!" I said. "Three 'short-*u*' sounds!"

To the teacher, however, this sentence on a worksheet was more than a phonics lesson gone blue. It was part of a growing body of evidence she brought to us to explain that something was wrong with Joseph Schwartz. Perhaps, to her mind, badly wrong.

They say a good teacher makes a difference, and the kindergarten teacher proved that. The first-grade teacher did, too, but in a different way.

Where the kindergarten teacher had been adaptable, this one

was rigid. If all the kids were doing phonics worksheets, then Joseph would have to do them too, even if he was already making a considerable dent in the public library's children's section and reading the Harry Potter series for the second or third time at home. (With more than one reading, he would calmly explain, "I can see the foreshadowing.") He got so bored in her class that he would wander over to the reading area, pull down a pile of books, and disappear.

Ms. First Grade was also a known quantity: during Sam's fifth-grade year at the school, she had been one of his teachers. It had not been a wonderful experience, but Sam, with his sturdy emotional armor, took everything in stride. Sam had not been shy in expressing his opinion of her at home, though. And Joseph, ever the soul of tact, came up to her one day early in the year and said, "My brother says you're not a good teacher."

Way to set the tone, little dude!

Joseph, with his growing list of problems and anger, was becoming a handful at school. While he wasn't disruptive in the classroom and got along with the other kids pretty well, pressure was building at points in the day that brought Joseph and the teacher into conflict. They soon had a full-scale battle of wills going on, with the teacher growing increasingly brittle over things that seemed almost trivial to us. The best teachers and smart parents learn that you have to pick your fights, but this teacher seemed to want to jump into all of them.

The most common battle occurred during the colder months, at recess, and at the end of the day. The children were required to put on their coats and wait to be led outside. The school was stuffy, and Joseph was miserable in his coat, so he would try to take it off and carry it. The teacher would order him to put it back on. It became a cycle of confrontation that was irritating to the teacher and Joseph alike, and it sent Joseph into a rage. The emotional burden from those confrontations spread into other parts of the day: as Jeanne pulled Joe's T-shirts out of his dresser in the mornings, she noticed that many of them had holes in the front; she realized that he was chewing on his shirts out of tension.

The teacher was getting angry, too. One day when Jeanne walked to the school to pick Joseph up, the kids were arrayed along an outdoor stairway waiting for dismissal. When he saw Jeanne, Joseph dropped his lunch box over the banister and it tumbled several feet to the ground below. To Jeanne's astonishment, the teacher started screaming. "Did you see that? He did that on purpose!" Whether or not Joseph had intentionally dropped the lunch box, the reaction seemed so out of proportion to the offense—and as Jeanne picked up the unbroken lunch box she couldn't help but wonder: *Who's the child here? Where's the grown-up?*

At parent-teacher conferences, or in quick asides when Jeanne volunteered at the school or picked Joe up at the end of the day, the teacher often took the opportunity to bring up her concern of the moment.

Some of the teacher's complaints were about real problems, but we disagreed on the underlying meaning. She told us that he sat too close to the girls in class, and he sometimes played with their hair. The teacher saw a child with boundary issues; we saw one who was fascinated by the girls and their hair and clothes. Eventually we would talk to a parent of another gay child who told us that her son had also gotten in trouble for touching girls' hair.

The teacher's most persistent complaint was that he was not paying attention in class. His habit of pulling down books and going off to a corner to read during class clearly bothered her; she said he was using the books to block her out. She acknowledged to Jeanne that the class often covered topics that Joseph already understood, but she saw the reading as worrisome mental detachment.

This wasn't the Joseph we saw at home, where he was engaged and always up for conversation, often about the books we were all reading. He didn't like starting his homework, of course—none of our kids was the type to simply sit down and get to work in their elementary school years, and this school's homework could take them hours to complete. Jeanne had a rule, though: you sit at the dining room table until your work is done. The kids complained, sometimes loudly, but the work always got done.

The teacher kept bringing up problems and hinting at deeper diagnoses. She noted that the noise in the cafeteria sometimes overwhelmed him, that he would sit with his hands over his ears, crying—another sign, she seemed to be saying, that his sensory apparatus was off-kilter. The day that she brought up the sentence with the three short-u sounds, she passed other in-class assignments across the table to Jeanne. One of Joe's sentences read, "Food doesn't taste as good as it should." The teacher turned to Joseph, who was sitting there, squirming miserably, and asked him, "Why did you write this?" She seemed to be trying to decide whether Joseph was being mistreated at home or whether his perceptions were somehow distorted.

The conversation trailed off inconclusively. Jeanne, a bit rattled by the teacher's prying, gathered up Joseph and his seemingly incriminating papers and walked him home. Trying to help Joseph navigate the shoals, she told him to be less creative in his class assignments, using unimaginative sentences like "I like ice cream" and "The weather is nice."

At one point, the teacher suggested that Joe should be checked for attention deficit hyperactivity disorder, ADHD. On still another visit, the teacher's veiled suggestion was a condition on the autism spectrum. "He doesn't look me in the eye when I talk to him," she said. But Joseph always looked us in the eye. Jeanne was trying to be polite, took it all in, and did not say what was on her mind: you intimidate and belittle him to his face, and then you criticize him for not looking you in the eye?

Isn't it possible, we thought, that a teacher who insists on giving a strong reader like Joe busywork on phonics simply might not be holding his attention? Is it possible that Sammy's comment to Joseph had been right—that this teacher simply isn't very good at her job?

The teacher had no training in psychology or medicine, but she had a problem in the classroom and an active imagination. Nothing she brought to us seemed severe enough, or well defined enough, to suggest a diagnosable condition. Her diagnosis-of-the-week approach was making it increasingly easy to dismiss her as alarmist. To us it seemed that this teacher, frustrated with her inability to get more cooperation out of Joseph, was trying to find a diagnosis to explain that the fault lay in him, not her. And if it was a problem that could be fixed with a pill, she seemed to be thinking, so much the better.

Jeanne and I didn't understand it at the time, but we were standing at the edge of a battlefield, encountering the first of a series of diagnoses from educators and medical professionals that would leave us dizzy. Even then, we were wary of the tendency of people to jump to conclusions about hyperactivity and other conditions. An occupational therapist who had worked with Sam in Maryland to improve his coordination recommended that he be tested for ADHD, since she believed the motor-spatial problems that she was treating him for tended to go hand in hand with attention deficit problems. We decided not to follow up, since the school had never complained that he was disruptive or overactive. Over time, our gut instinct proved correct—a fact confirmed by Sam's excellent college grades.

A battle is raging over whether or not doctors overdiagnose conditions like ADHD and overprescribe drugs for it, with the enthusiastic support of schools and parents as well. One camp says that lazy doctors and neurotic, overachieving parents follow the lead of the greedy drug companies and give drugs to kids who might be better off without them. The opposing side points to the success of pharmaceutical treatments for many people and the lack of effective mental health care for much of the population, and says if anything, psychoactive drugs are underprescribed.

No study I've found conclusively proves either side is right. But it's clear that some misdiagnosis occurs, and that many schools like the idea that a magic pill can solve their problems, or at least tranquilize the child into submission. Those schools want a pharmaceutical cure for a condition that, in some cases, might best be described as being a pain in the butt.

A backlash against the use of drugs like Ritalin is well under way. In an essay in the *New York Times* in January 2012, L. Alan Sroufe, a professor emeritus of psychology at the University of

Minnesota's Institute of Child Development, wrote that attention deficit drugs "increase concentration in the short term, which is why they work so well for college students cramming for exams. But when given to children over long periods of time, they neither improve school achievement nor reduce behavior problems." Since the drugs have "serious side effects" like stunting growth, he called for a reexamination of how readily we medicate our children for problems with focusing, and whether other issues might be the underlying cause. "Many of these children have anxiety or depression; others are showing family stresses," he wrote. "We need to treat them as individuals."[13]

Alison Gopnik, a professor of psychology at the University of California at Berkeley, discussed the ongoing fight over medicalization and medication in a 2010 essay in the online magazine *Slate*. She was reviewing *We've Got Issues: Children and Parents in the Age of Medication*, a book by Judith Warner that argues the medical interventions are, for the most part, necessary and helpful. Gopnik wrote that antipsychotic drugs and antidepressants help many people. Other conditions, she explained, are not so readily unlocked with a pharmaceutical key: "Syndromes like autism, ADHD, or dyslexia are like 'fever,' or 'dropsy,' rather than like malaria or polio," she wrote. "They are names for somewhat incoherent collections of symptoms rather than clearly identified causes. Other 'diseases' like 'childhood bipolar disorder' or 'sensory integration disorder' are even less clearly defined and may exist only in the minds of the therapists."

Gopnik wrote that it is easy to sympathize with parents who want to do something to help their children, "but that doesn't alter the fact that the scientific evidence just isn't clear about what to do. On balance, though, the evidence suggests that we should be conservative about prescribing drugs to children, and much more conservative than we actually are." Gopnik ended the essay with a strong push for cognitive behavioral therapies, which can be effective for a wide range of psychological problems and which, "unlike drugs, do no harm."[14]

We do know families whose children's lives have been changed immeasurably for the better by an accurate diagnosis and the judicious use of medications for a range of conditions that include attention deficit and bipolar disorder. "We got our daughter back," a colleague whose daughter had ADHD told me happily.

If Joseph did, after careful evaluation, turn out to have a condition severe enough that it required medication, and if the medication was effective for the condition, we wouldn't hesitate to get him that treatment, just as we'd start a course of insulin if a checkup showed diabetes. And eventually, meds would be part of Joseph's life, at least for a while. But we had a wariness of snap judgment and unwarranted faith in diagnoses. We wanted to be sure, especially when considering conditions like Asperger's syndrome and others on the autism spectrum. A faction of the clinical community believes that early diagnosis and treatment of conditions on the autism spectrum are essential to keep neurologically influenced behavior from becoming unbreakable habits. But what if Joseph didn't need medical intervention in order to grow and develop?

Over time, the drumbeat of diagnoses would become louder and more insistent, with a growing suggestion that Joseph's difficulties interacting with people placed him somewhere on the autism spectrum. We understood that to many people, our reluctance to put Joseph in a diagnostic box made us seem out of step. But there are experts who feel the way we do. Alex Weintrob, a former president of the American Society for Adolescent Psychiatry, seemed to echo our thoughts in a February 2010 letter to the *New York Times* in response to a story about diagnoses. He wrote that "at least until a child reaches late adolescence, we should be very careful before assigning a diagnosis of autism spectrum disorder or Asperger's disorder. In more than forty years of practice as a child psychiatrist, I have found it more fair and reasonable to 'label' someone as a 'quirky kid' who may need some social training skills, rather than offering a medical diagnosis."[15]

I called Dr. Weintrob recently, and he explained that there can be benefits to a medical diagnosis for a patient: "it gives him some structure" to understanding the problem, and it can open the doors to treatment, insurance coverage, and school services. At the same time, he warned, there is a risk as well— of "pathologizing, and making the kid feel there's something wrong with his brain." And so, he said, "I'm on the side of great concern about pathologizing behavior that we don't know what the hell it's all about."

A teacher or clinician, he said, might suspect Asperger's in a youngster who can't meet his gaze, but "maybe he doesn't look you in the eye because he doesn't look you in the eye," he said.

"In forty-plus years, I've learned what I don't know."

Bearing up under the continuing conflict and the stream of suggested diagnoses, we decided to simply wait Joe's teacher out. Spring had come, and the school year would end before long. We could all get through it.

Ms. First Grade did bring up something we thought we could do something about: Joe's handwriting. She complained that it was nearly illegible and suggested that we get him occupational therapy, which addresses coordination issues. Jeanne set up a series of regular appointments. The therapist suggested we keep coming through the end of the school year to help him gain the confidence to write well in the classroom. Jeanne was happy to have a regular excuse to get him away from a teacher who made him miserable.

At home, Joseph was still, for the most part, the playful, happy child who could get lost in a book or make a sneaky raid on his sister's jewelry box. But the conflicts at school were beginning to come home. After so many notes and calls from the school, Jeanne had asked in frustration, "What do you want me to do?" The school responded that she should convince him to comply with his teacher's demands.

When Jeanne took that approach, Joseph's face fell. He had felt that he was under attack at school, but home was a safe haven. She decided that Joseph needed her support more than the school did, and we hoped that things would improve as he moved on to more understanding teachers.

Some teachers would prove more supportive, but over time the conflict and gloom would accumulate. The confident child who skipped his way to kindergarten would be supplanted by a darker boy who slouched his way home after another day of failure.

CHAPTER FOUR

"Raising a child isn't complicated, love. It isn't easy, but it isn't complicated, either."

She tilted her head, looking up at him. "How's it done, then?"

He shrugged. "You just love them more than air and water and light. From there, everything else comes naturally."

—JIM BUTCHER, *PRINCEPS' FURY*[16]

If only it were that easy, this whole loving them "more than air and water and light." Count Bernard, the character who says those words in Jim Butcher's high-fantasy series of novels, never had to sit down with a child study team or discuss *u*-sounds with a disapproving, suspicious teacher. But he's right about one thing: love is the starting point. Without that, nothing else works.

By second grade, Joseph wasn't just getting into conflicts with teachers. He was starting to skirmish with some of the other kids as well.

As the school year began, I walked Joseph the couple of blocks up to the redbrick school. The children had separated into groups at the picnic benches out front, with girls chatting at one bench and boys horsing around near another. Joseph ran briefly with the boys but was ignored. When he drifted over to the girls' table and sat down to talk, the girls turned to face one another, freezing him out.

The second-grade teacher was young and pleasant and gave out candies as rewards to the kids. She was all about positive reinforcement, and Joseph liked her. But he was still rattled from the previous year's harangues, and it began to play out in conflict with classmates. One day early in second grade, the teacher found him backed into a corner, holding a thumbtack as if to defend himself against the other children. She had no sense of what the others had been doing, but his sense of isolation, anxiety, and occasional bursts of anger worried her. Of course, it worried us, too. We wondered what could have been going through his mind in that tight corner. Something, whether real or imagined, was making him afraid of his schoolmates.

The teacher's warmth boosted his spirits, at least initially. She had a positive approach to problems. Joseph had a tendency to get frequent nosebleeds, real gushers. His doctor advised a wait-and-see approach, but while we waited he was bleeding all over the place. This teacher saw the episodes as a way to organize the class and try to teach them compassion. Whenever Joe's nose started to bleed, a rotating EMT squad of kids would spring into action, grabbing the Kleenex, pressing the tissues against Joe's nose, and escorting him to the nurse.

Joe's happy flamboyant streak still showed through here and there. At-home projects got heavy glitter treatment. In one report, Joseph referred to Saladin, the first sultan of Egypt and Syria, as "the fabulous Muslim leader." Apparently, Joe was very impressed with a biography's images of the twelfth-century figure in all his finery.

As the year progressed, however, the teacher seemed to get overwhelmed with the daily grind of school, and she had less energy to deal with Joseph's problems and moods. His anger was close to the surface, and meltdowns were growing more common. Some students made a game of making him blow up, like the boy who would enrage Joseph by calling him "Lemon-head" every time he wore his yellow raincoat. The boy knew that the kid who goes ape is the one that gets into trouble, rarely the instigator—especially if the reaction seems to be out of proportion to the provocation. Other kids would hide his sweatshirt at recess, day after day, to see him fall apart when he couldn't find it. Each outburst humiliated him more.

Was it a tough school? Not at all. The schools we had left behind in Takoma Park had far more frequent incidents of physical bullying, and Joe's older brother, Sam, had learned to defend himself against kids who knocked him into lockers and even shoved him into a urinal, drenching him. One especially troubled boy at Sam's school knocked a bird's nest out of a limb on school property and stomped a baby bird to death.

When we got to town, Sam spent his first week at the elementary school and asked us suspiciously, "Did you send me to a private school?" He explained that when the teacher had asked the kids to describe their summer vacations, they had spoken of their trips to Europe. And, he said, "the biggest discipline problem we've got is a kid who talks without raising his hand."

Joe's group wasn't completely docile. One day, a boy threw

him into some tables at the school cafeteria. On another, three kids jumped on him on his way home from school as he carried his rented violin. Joseph went into a rage, flinging his little body around and hitting them with the violin case. The kids scattered.

When Joe got home from being jumped, he told Jeanne the boys' names. She knew them from the neighborhood and felt they weren't actually bad kids. Some parents in our position might sound the alarm and scream for blood; we decided not to follow up with the school or their parents. We wanted to see if Joe's act of self-defense had been enough to get the boys to back off, since that's how things had worked for Sammy. When Sam finally stood up for himself during his Takoma Park days and threw the kid who had been bullying him the most against a wall, the harassment stopped. Compared to what we had seen in Maryland, our scale for trouble was set pretty high. Kids do stupid things, and we were tired of hearing about every infraction of Joseph's from the school. We didn't want to feed the cycles of recrimination. Besides, Joe had come home that day flush with triumph.

Sure enough, Joseph wasn't attacked physically again by those kids. But the taunts, and the shunning, continued. Resilient Sam had been able to slough off the rambunctious obnoxiousness of other schoolkids. But Joseph, more sensitive and vulnerable by nature, continued to stew. When furiously upset, he began to bite the back of his hand. His teeth never broke the skin, but the deep marks were unnerving to teachers.

On stressful days, Joseph would cry in the school lunchroom, pulling his hoodie over his head so that it wouldn't be obvious. Instead of trying to comfort him, the lunchroom aides insisted that wearing a hat in the building was against school rules and ordered him to pull the hood back down, driving him to more furious tears.

Ms. Second Grade suggested psychotherapy to help Joseph master his behavior. In a conversation with Jeanne, she said, "Intellectually, he's *here*," and raised her hand well above her head. She dropped her other hand to waist level and continued, "But emotionally, he's here." She confided apologetically to Jeanne that Joseph had gotten bad luck of the draw when it came to classmates. "These kids aren't as accepting as the ones I had last year," she said. "If this had been the class from last year, they would have treated him better."

She seemed to be losing patience with this vulnerable boy. Jeanne, on a visit to the school one day, saw that Joseph, at the back of a line, was being teased by another boy until he cried. By the time his teacher noticed, Joseph's emotions were so out of control that he was unable to even tell her what the other boy had done. The teacher had two dozen other kids to deal with; she threw up her hands.

On another day, Jeanne called the teacher to complain about the lost sweatshirts, the "Lemonhead" taunts, and other harassment at recess. The teacher said that the other kids admitted to having hidden Joe's clothes and calling him names but said that he called them names as well. "Isn't anyone supervising the playground?" Jeanne asked in frustration.

Abruptly, the teacher lowered her voice and whispered into the phone, "He's at risk of being *classified*—don't you think that's the worst possible thing that could happen to him?"

Jeanne told me about the conversation when I got home; we were both taken aback. As many problems as Joseph was having at school, we had seen them as more of a rough patch than a psychological crisis. And, since we were unaccustomed to the language and rules of the school disability system, we were confused. What did classification even mean? The teacher's urgent warning seemed to suggest exclusion and a narrowing of options, or perhaps something embarrassing or even punishing. But it gave us little sense of what it might mean in practical terms for a kid like Joe.

I called the principal to ask what this talk of classification was all about, but he waved me off with a vague comment that the decision to start that process was up to him, and implied that he wasn't pursuing it at that time. The school remained a black box to parents like us; we only heard what Joseph told us, or what teachers might let slip. The principal seemed to be saying that he would tell us the school's plans for Joseph once they had come to a decision, but that we weren't a part of that process. Meanwhile, the misunderstandings and mistrust were compounded.

It would be a while before we understood that classification begins the process of identifying a child as having a disability or behavioral problem. For children with big deficiencies, classification can lead to being pulled out of the mainstream of the school. But it also can set beneficial services and accommodations in motion. Had we known more, for example, we might have been able to get Joseph the services of the school district's special education physical therapist during gym. Without those services, he irked the coach by showing as much resistance to sports and games as he had during that first moment on the peewee soccer field. The coach saw defiance. But we later came to understand from a physical education teacher with special ed training that participating in sports was especially hard for Joseph, because he lacked the motor skills to take part and the social skills to deal with teamwork. The physical therapist could have helped him fulfill his state requirement for physical education while building his coordination and abilities—not preparing him to play football or lacrosse but at least getting him involved in healthy activity. Instead, he was engaged in an unnecessary battle of wills with coaches that lasted for years.

Classification also could have broken open the black box of the school. The federal law governing education for children with disabilities, the Individuals with Disabilities Education Act, requires regular meetings to determine an Individual Education Plan with a child study team that works together to find the best strategies for the child. Under a system like that, teachers could have been warned about the toxic nature of entering a battle of wills with Joseph. Testing might have uncovered the problems with handwriting that led people to think Joseph was lazy or mulish when, in fact, he found writing anything by hand a struggle. Instead, everyone just muddled along, and we were thankful at the end of each year and hopeful about the next, with the increasing sense that we were like Charlie Brown, trapped in a Sisyphean cycle of running at Lucy's football.

By that point, there had been enough troubling incidents at school that we took the step the second-grade teacher had recommended and found a psychotherapist. Joe's anger was flaring, and we were receiving a growing number of notes about his role in playground squabbles. We hoped he would benefit from therapy. But we also felt that the teacher and the school would back off a bit if they saw that we were taking action to address his problems.

The therapist we found was sweet and inviting. She said nothing about attention deficit disorder or the other conditions darkly hinted at by teachers without a fraction of her clinical training. Instead, she said that Joseph was a boy with social problems that she could help him to address. They played games with dolls, working through their interactions with each other, and Joe looked forward to the visits. He had missed his Barbies.

After a couple of happy months with the therapist, we decided it was time to ask our big question: Was Joe gay? We had hesitated to even bring it up, wondering whether it might seem weird or even creepy for us to be talking about the sexual orientation of an eight-year-old. But increasingly, we were wondering if sexual orientation could be part of what separated him from the other kids—whether it might help explain his problems with fitting in and be a source of much of the stress he was under. If it was part of his problems, we felt it was important to get a measure of confirmation and whatever advice she could give. So we summoned our courage, walked into her office one day without Joseph, and nervously told her that we believed that he might be gay.

"What a terrible thing to say about your son," she responded.

We were too startled even to ask what she'd meant. The response felt like a slap. It had taken a lot of effort just to ask, to overcome our own waffling about whether we were seeing signals or insignificant affectations. Now she seemed to be saying that we were bad parents for even bringing up the question, and that our concerns weren't worth talking about. The rebuff made us even more reluctant to talk about Joe's sexual orientation with authority figures for some time.

We hadn't yet heard of the "sissy boy" research, and it appeared that she hadn't either. The fact that he loved dolls and liked walking around the house in the pink feather boa that he had begged for in the crafts store, after all, could just be a swerve on the way to heterosexual adulthood—just as Sam's Halloween ball gown had been a simple lark. We certainly weren't ready to be convinced yet that our Joey might be gay, despite the accumulating number of Big Honking Clues.

So we let the matter drop, and Jeanne kept bringing Joseph to the sessions through the end of that school year. At that point the therapist said that he was doing well, and that he had stocked up his little toolbox of techniques for dealing with stress and social situations, and suggested the course of treatment was at an end.

She wasn't the only therapist Joe saw that year. The conflicts with the gym teacher had us thinking that we should add to the growing army of specialists by taking Joseph to a different kind of occupational therapist who would focus on his gross motor skills.

Jeanne was hoping to repeat the good experience with occupational therapy that had helped Sammy so much. We'd started Sam in occupational therapy because his handwriting was also illegible, and because he was so maladroit that if he leaned over in a chair to pick up his backpack, he was likely to fall over. Teachers thought he was clowning, but it all came down to balance and coordination. He had trouble riding a bike as well. The specialist worked with Sam, using techniques that seemed almost nutty—hoisting him into the air on ropes and harnesses and telling him to stab hoops with lances. But within a few months, he was wheeling around the neighborhood on his bike and asking to try out for soccer. He was a boy transformed.

With a success like that in our recent past, we went looking for someone to help Joseph. A highly recommended therapist brought him into her office for a couple of weeks of testing. When she was done, she told us that his fine motor coordination was good. That was no surprise to us, since he'd been playing piano for a couple of years, and his fingers flew across the keyboard. She also correctly noted several signs of poor body awareness, for example his tendency to lead with the wrong foot when throwing a ball. These problems could be corrected with exercises. That seemed promising.

But then she announced she had come to a conclusion about Joe's underlying issue and a prominent feature of her recommended treatment: "He needs to be brushed."

Say what?

She had diagnosed Joseph with a condition known as sensory integration dysfunction, or more recently as sensory processing disorder. Running a soft brush against his skin on a daily basis would reduce his sensitivity to stimulation, she said. It would help with mother-and-son bonding, too. He'd also need, she said, a special pad at his desk at school that he could kick against. He could brush himself at school, she explained; many kids with the disorder just step into a closet and use the brush to steady themselves.

This called for more research at home. It did appear that her diagnosis might describe some problems that Joseph had, especially his meltdowns in the cafeteria. The transition from the quiet orderliness of kindergarten, when the children ate together in the classroom, to the noise and chaos of the elementary school lunchroom had been rough on him, as it had been on some of the other kids. The first-grade teacher had even recommended that Joseph be fitted with earmuffs that would cancel the noise, a recommendation we did not follow up on.

In other ways, the diagnosis didn't seem to fit the symptoms I found online at all: Joseph didn't find certain clothes unbearable to the touch, and he didn't make frustrating demands about the kinds of food that he would eat. And he didn't avoid hugs; he craved them.

My research showed more. Many parents swore by the treatment, but the expensive therapies were still unproven, and some are controversial within the medical community—especially brushing. And while many broadly accepted treatments have first gone through a phase of being considered heretical by the medical establishment, sometimes the medical establishment is right. This time, it seemed to me, it was.

The therapist had checked Joseph's eye-tracking abilities, a diagnostic tool in the field, and had noticed his eyes were slightly askew. This, we knew. I'd had strabismus as a boy, and gotten two operations at Joseph's age to keep from growing as wall-eyed as Jean-Paul Sartre. So we had been quick to notice the slight strabismus in Joe's eyes, and doctors had looked as well. No one thought it was anything more than a mild case, and his ophthalmologist told us the alignment corrected itself when Joe wore glasses.

But the occupational therapist warned us that the condition would have to be addressed, or it might slow Joseph's development as a reader.

Joseph. Trouble reading? Right. That's when we knew that while she had gotten many things about Joseph correct, she did not have all the answers for him.

On one visit during the testing and evaluation phase, I struck up a conversation with a mom in the waiting room. I asked whether she thought her daughter was benefiting from techniques like brushing. She smiled knowingly. "The brushing is pretty silly," she said. "But she likes coming here, and I think the exercises do help."

After those initial few weeks, we decided not to follow up. Sam had jousted in the air in the privacy of a therapist's office. The idea that Joseph might be at school kicking his pad and ducking into the closet for a brushing break, or wearing special earmuffs in the lunchroom to block out the noise, left us thinking he would seem even weirder to his teachers and classmates than he already did.

It was not the first time that a medical professional seemed to be offering what felt like a one-size-fits-all diagnosis. It reminded me of the famous scene from Joseph Heller's *Catch-22*, with Yossarian watching doctors examining a patient with a mysterious condition. ("I see everything twice!")

> *A colonel with a large forehead and horn-rimmed glasses soon arrived at a diagnosis.*
>
> *"It's meningitis," he called out emphatically, waving the others back. "Although Lord knows there's not the slightest reason for thinking so."*
>
> *"Then why pick meningitis?" inquired a major with a suave chuckle. "Why not, let's say, acute nephritis?"*
>
> *"Because I'm a meningitis man, that's why, and not an acute-nephritis man," retorted the colonel.*[17]

At that point, we had taken Joseph to two therapists for motor skills, with the result that our son still couldn't tie his shoes properly and did anything he could to sit out P.E. It was depressing and expensive. We didn't know how we would cope with middle school, where the pressure to participate in gym would probably be even greater. But we decided to give occupational therapy a rest, at least for a while.

By third grade, things were starting to look up. Joe's teacher was lovable and had a great hand with him. She instantly grasped that this was a kid who could make a contribution in class; he could be persuaded with firm friendliness, but coercion would turn him obstinate.

He was more comfortable in her classroom. He kept up with the homework and was fully engaged in class discussion and even chatting with the girls again. But his troubles with handwriting seemed to be getting worse. When he tried to write anything longer than what was required to complete a short-answer quiz, the tip of his pencil would often force through the paper and tear it; the tip would snap, requiring a sharpener. It both frustrated him and broke his concentration. He all but stopped writing in class.

This teacher didn't call him lazy; instead, she looked for solutions. She worked persistently and patiently with him until he ground out the major assignment of the year with her, an illustrated book. It took a lot of time and effort on both of their parts, but when Joseph completed it, her praise was enthusiastic and heartfelt.

She asked Jeanne to bring in an egg timer so that she could set deadlines for Joseph to do his work, a technique that had once worked with another reluctant writer. That didn't help, so she asked what Jeanne's secret was for getting Joe to work at home. Jeanne pointed out that the work was typed, and explained that Joe did his work quickly when seated at a keyboard. There wasn't a computer in the class for him to use to complete assignments, however. He and the teacher ultimately reached an impasse and he did little more written work in class that year. Still, we got no reports of angry outbursts, and he came home talking happily about the school day.

We had come to realize that he was still something of a work in progress—emphasis on work—but was headed in the right direction. We must be past the worst, right?

Ms. Third Grade suggested yet another form of therapy: speech therapy. Joseph had long had a lisp, but recently he had begun to stammer and developed a kind of "uhnn" sound that slipped into sentences.

So: speech therapy. Why not? Jeanne asked the teacher, "I could do this with a private therapist instead, right?" Jeanne was still worried about the implications of the mysterious "classification" that would be required to apply for services, and how it would be reflected in his record. The teacher set her straight: "Why do that when you can get the services for free?" This was a straightforward and specific service, provided by the school, she explained. Benign. Do it.

And she was right. The school had a gifted speech therapist on staff—a wisecracking, bubbly Jersey girl who Joseph came immediately to love and trust. It was a connection that would prove vital before long.

Lisping gave Joseph something in common with David Sedaris, whose accounts of growing up gay have entertained millions of readers. He told the story of his own elementary school speech therapy sessions in his memoir *Me Talk Pretty One Day*, with the keen eye that did not miss the big clue that lisping contained.[18]

For one thing, he noticed, there weren't any girls getting the treatment. "They were all boys like me who kept movie star scrapbooks and made their own curtains. 'You don't want to be doing that,' the men in our families would say. 'That's a girl thing.'"

The speech therapist, he wrote, talked about putting a sign on her door. "She was probably thinking along the lines of SPEECH THERAPY LAB, though a more appropriate marker would have read FUTURE HOMOSEXUALS OF AMERICA."

Sedaris said that the gay boys didn't just try to master their speech. They tried to fit in, as well. As he put it, "We learned to be duplicitous." That meant hiding their effeminate side. "Our stacks of *Cosmopolitan* were topped with an unread issue of *Boys' Life* or *Sports Illustrated*, and our decoupage projects were concealed beneath the sporting equipment we never asked for but always received."

Sedaris made it hilarious. Joseph was starting to hide himself, too, but it wasn't funny.

Coming up through elementary school, many kids feel pressure to conform, and Joseph was no exception. By third grade, there were no class reports on "fabulous" Saladin. Jeanne noticed that Joseph examined her face closely for reactions to his word choices, and that he seemed startled when she smiled with amusement at words like "fabulous" and "prettiful." Those words quickly dropped out of his vocabulary as he edited his speech and, seemingly, his persona. He altered his walk from a loose sashay to a more controlled stride. In his room, the feather boa became a nest for one of his ceramic birds; not discarded but tucked away.

For years, Joseph's most flamboyant time came in December, when we'd haul out the fake Christmas tree and let him take the lead in decorating it. Jeanne is a lapsed Catholic, and as a Jew growing up in the South, I didn't have *tannenbaum* phobia that so many of my Jewish friends who were raised in the Northeast seem to have. She likes to joke that the tree means more to me than it does to her.

Joseph would make it magnificent, with ornaments sent up by the grandparents and which he collected during the year, including our kids' art projects from Sunday school at the temple over the years. He hung everything shiny and prettiful on that tree, and looked forward to decorating it long after his brother and sister had lost interest.

That third-grade year, though, decorating the tree was a more subdued affair. To us, he seemed almost guilty about it.

As the sissy boy studies and similar work by other researchers show, it's natural for effeminate kids to butch up a bit as they become conscious of the ways and attitudes of those around them. But further research suggests that hiding that side of themselves can come at a high price.

Ilan H. Meyer, a senior scholar for public policy at the Williams Institute for Sexual Orientation Law and Public Policy at UCLA's School of Law, has focused on this problem as part of his research into the psychological pressures felt by sexual minorities. I'll go into greater depth about his work later, but it's worth bringing up one of the most powerful ideas he writes about: "minority stress," or the discomfort that comes from being different. Pressure can be caused by encounters with actual prejudice, but the pressure can also be internal, coming from what Meyer calls "expectations of rejection and discrimination," and from concealing sexual orientation. As he has put it, "There's a stress that's involved with concealing."

While the less girly Joe got fewer hassles for being different, the effort was causing new kinds of stress for him. It wasn't obvious, but maybe there were other signs. He immersed himself in role-playing games on the computer like Diablo II and Neverwinter Nights. Joseph almost always chose female characters, beautiful and deadly. Joe told me recently, "I remember wondering, in playing Diablo II, whether my character would be better suited by more powerful armor or prettier armor," and proudly recalled that he chose the prettier enhancements in shades of amethyst, acid green, and cobalt blue. Through his color-coordinated avatars, he slew demons by the thousands.

Not all demons are as easy to dispatch; even birthday parties could be fraught occasions. Joe's aversion to sports made his classmates' bowling and Rollerblading parties a poor fit. But he had always been excited about throwing his own birthday parties and inviting the other kids to come celebrate with him at the local art studio or the ceramics shop.

Then came his tenth birthday. He helped to plan the party and looked forward to it with excitement. When the big Saturday came, a good crowd showed up. It all seemed to come off well.

But when everybody got back to school on Monday, the boys had a question.

"Joseph, why did you have your party at *Build-A-Bear*? That's where *girls* have parties!"

It would be years before he asked for another birthday party.

CHAPTER FIVE

There's a widespread notion that children are open, that the truth about their inner selves just seeps out of them. That's all wrong. No one is more covert than a child, and no one has a greater need to be that way. It's a response to a world that's always using a can opener to open them up to see what's inside, wondering whether it ought to be replaced with a more useful sort of preserves.

—SMILLA'S SENSE OF SNOW[19]

Joseph, it was becoming increasingly clear, was a different kind of kid. He could be startlingly bright. But he was also unable to tie his shoes without a fumble-fingered struggle. He had flourished under the guidance of good teachers, but even in his happy third-grade year, he almost never put pencil to paper in class. Still, he seemed to be steadying, and promised Jeanne that fourth grade would be the year that he would try hard to focus in school and do the class work. We had seen from his experience in first grade, however, that a confrontational teacher could bruise his fragile sense of self.

The fourth-grade teacher would shatter it.

Mr. Fourth had been chosen for Joseph by the third-grade teacher, who discussed the choice with Jeanne and told her that the two seemed like a good match—or, at least, a better match than with the other two teachers. She considered one of them to be too much of a softie who wouldn't be able to get him to perform for her. The other, she said, might be too strict. Mr. Fourth had a reputation for having a sense of humor and engaging the class in discussion. His father had been a world-traveling anthropologist, and so his classroom was like a natural history museum, packed with animal skeletons and exotic objects from around the globe. Many of his students recalled him as one of their favorites. He was also considered a strong disciplinarian who finally might be able to get Joseph to produce class work.

In recent years, however, his life had suffered a series of reversals, including cancer. Joseph's older brother, Sam, had this teacher a few years before and had found him disorganized, domineering, and volatile; when frustrated, he was quick to yell at the kids. "He kind of squeezed the life out of things," Sam recalled.

Sam had noticed something else: this teacher singled out one or two boys for extra discipline and criticism throughout the year. During Sam's year, the child who was the focus of the teacher's attention, a decent kid, was ridden so hard that he started looking for any excuse to stay home from school. One day when the boy was absent, the teacher told the students that he had called the boy's mother at home to complain about him and to ask why he wasn't in school. Sam said the teacher shook his head and recounted with amazement that the mother had yelled at him.

It was as if the targeted kids were the scapegoats for the class, and the teacher used them to unite the rest of the group.

A neighbor's son inadvertently revealed the effect, telling us one day that the teacher "is great—but there were a couple of really bad kids in the class!" If you weren't the goat, apparently, the experience was great. Fall within his spotlight, however, and the result was misery for the child and his parents as well.

Other teachers had wondered how Mr. Fourth chose the kids he picked on. One would later tell me, "he didn't want to be bothered with anybody who was different."

The years since Sam had been in Mr. Fourth's class had continued to be difficult for the teacher, with more surgical procedures to address the after-effects of the cancer treatments, including one just before the beginning of Joe's school year. He was living with weakened bones, muscle degeneration, and hearing loss, and seemed always to be hurting. The burden of illness would shave away many of his positive attributes as a teacher and bring out his worst.

But for the first two months of school, while the teacher was absent and recovering from the surgery, a substitute teacher ran the class. She had the gift of being able to hold kids to high standards while being supportive. The class was well behaved under her authority, and Joseph got things done for her. Her method wasn't magical. One day she assigned some in-class work that Joseph had not completed. She told him firmly that he had to do it, so he sat down, dashed off the work, and handed it to her. She told him that wasn't good enough and calmly had him do it again. When he turned that in, she called for still another try: "You'll do it over recess." He sat through part of recess with her and redid the work. When he finally turned in work that she declared herself satisfied with, it was a triumph for them both.

That idyll ended when Mr. Fourth returned. At an early parent-teacher conference with him, it sounded like he had gotten a thorough briefing from Ms. First, the teacher with all of the diagnoses for Joe. Mr. Fourth said he saw Joseph as a project for the year: he was going to train him to look him in the eye when he spoke and to be still in class. It would later become obvious that this meant he had chosen Joseph as one of the two class goats.

The teacher began to press Joseph and another boy, the only Hispanic child in the class, relentlessly. Joseph, initially fearful, quickly became angry. When the teacher shouted, he shouted back. Trips to the principal for time-outs, notes sent home, and calls from the office became regular occurrences.

Sometimes the discipline got physical. "I went to school one day to tell Joseph not to forget to go to his after-school class," Jeanne remembered. "I was early, so I waited in the hallway. As I sat there, the bell rang, and Joseph started for the door. The teacher told another kid to block the door and grabbed Joseph and held on to him, while I watched, unobserved from the hallway. After all of the other children were gone, he let Joseph go. I was sick to my stomach," Jeanne recalled. "My son was being treated like an animal."

Other teachers had used calm and steady persuasion, which had worked. This bullying was a disaster. One of the crossing guards down the street from the school stopped Jeanne to ask why Joseph, who had always talked to her happily at the corner, was now rushing by with his head down every day, upset. "What is that teacher doing?" she asked, troubled. "Joseph's a good kid."

I took our concerns to the principal and asked him to move Joseph to another class. I argued that he wouldn't be subjected to a daily power struggle, and the obviously ill teacher would get a break as well. He sighed and told me it was against the school's policy to transfer kids from one teacher to another: "We almost never do that." All of his teachers, he calmly explained, were "certified and qualified." To the principal, we were trying to micromanage his domain, and Joseph was the problem, not the teacher. He seemed to be saying that we were making things worse by standing up for our kid. I asked repeatedly over the course of that year, but the principal, always politely, refused to budge.

He was acting in part out of sympathy for a man struggling with serious illness. We shared that feeling, but we couldn't ignore what he was doing to our child. Joseph's school picture from that year shows a boy, mouth slightly open, eyes wide and round, staring blankly into the camera: lost. One day when a school staffer came in, she observed Joseph on the floor of the classroom. He was, she said, rolling around on the floor and licking a table leg.

That's how they reported it to us, anyway. When we asked Joseph about it, he didn't remember having done it. He said that all the kids had been on the floor that day; the teacher often had them sit on the floor for classroom exercises. It was, to us, baffling. The objects in our home were resolutely unlicked. But some at the school seized on this incident as a sign of deep neurological disturbance.

Like the first-grade teacher, Mr. Fourth had diagnoses in mind—though, wary of school policies against offering them directly, he would hint broadly. One day he called the house with a question about the recent round of eye tests given at the school. Joseph had turned out to be severely nearsighted, and it looked like he would start wearing glasses that year. I'd gotten my first pair in fourth grade as well, so this came as no surprise.

To the teacher, however, it seemed to be an answer—a big reason Joseph wasn't doing work in class. If he couldn't read the chalkboard, he might be dropping out of the flow of the class. Right?

Jeanne assured him that we would be seeing the ophthalmologist soon and getting glasses for him. Then the teacher carried the conversation further, and started hinting that the problems he was having with Joseph in class must be seated in mental illness or a spectrum disorder—he seemed to be comparing Joseph to another child in the school who was autistic, as if their conditions were identical. Jeanne disagreed with the comparison, and his voice rose in frustration. "You know what the problem is, Mrs. Schwartz," he said. Jeanne was confused; she didn't know what he meant, and he didn't seem willing to get more explicit. Jeanne tried to explain that a psychologist had observed Joseph carefully in second grade and found nothing wrong with him.

"If she said that," the teacher shouted into the phone, "then she must be *crazy*!"

Over time, he would complain that Joseph looked at him in a threatening way. One day, he said ominously, Joseph pointed his pencil at him, muttering.

At home, we started to wonder which of them was more disturbed.

While Joseph was dealing with new pressures from the outside, he had growing stress on the inside, too. He was in turmoil over what he called "the secret."

To us, the secret seemed to be no secret at all. That fall, I had checked the browser history on the computer Joseph used—something I had done occasionally with the older kids as well. Before you call me Big Brother, let me explain:

I'm the Dad. I get to do this.

We didn't try to censor our children's use of the Internet, a fool's errand if ever there was one. But we did make sure they weren't getting themselves into trouble with strangers or putting themselves at risk by divulging personal information. I didn't want my kids receiving or sending cyberbullying e-mails and instant messages. And, since I was writing quite a bit about online piracy at the time, I was keeping an eye out for illicit downloading. Being sued by the music industry I was covering would have been, um, inconvenient.

When I quietly checked Sam's browser history when he was age twelve, I found what I expected to see sooner or later: images of naked women, and of naked women having sex with naked men.

When I checked Joseph's browser history during his fourth-grade year, there were plenty of naked people as well. But all of the images were of men. If we were still wondering about Joseph's sexual orientation, the time for wondering was over. Browsers don't lie.

Joseph, however, was not ready to tell us anything about this. In talking about those days recently, he explained to me that he had actually figured out his sexual orientation even earlier, at the age of eight.

As he told the tale, his personal revelation was purely twenty-first century. "I was on Wikipedia," he said, "and somehow I found out what homosexuality was." At that moment online, he realized something startling. "I thought, 'Eww. Boys like *girls*?' So I decided that research was merited."

That research was elegant in its simplicity. "I looked at pictures of naked men and pictures of naked women, and figured out which I liked better." With that issue resolved, he said, "it sort of got shoved to the back of my mind." It was if he told himself, "I don't care about it at this point; I'll care about it later."

Now that his teacher was delivering a daily message to him in the classroom that there seemed to be something seriously wrong with him, Joseph's secret—the thing that made him different from the kids around him—became another source of torment. His browser history showed he was viewing Web pages about the risks of online sex sites, full of scary, dire warnings about the perils of the virtual world. It all dovetailed with his feelings of anguish over school and was driving him deeper into himself.

I came into his room one night to broach the subject of the secret, and to ask whether he was seeing things online that troubled him. "I don't want to talk about it," he said urgently.

"But you'll come to me when you do?" I asked. He said that he would. I tried, haltingly, clumsily, to drop a hint that we knew what was going on. "You know, Joseph, you can always tell me when something's bothering you. We love you no matter what—"

"Please. Leave," he said.

By the end of the fall semester at school, Joseph was a mess; over the Christmas break we took a family trip to Texas, and he had several meltdowns. At a dinner in Austin with one of my aunts, a painter whose work portrayed the naked bodies of women with the heads of wolves and other animals, Joseph lost it. "The art is freaking me out!" he shouted, and stayed on the deck behind her house until it was time to go. He said the images haunted him for a long time after.

He was emotionally vulnerable and easily spooked. During our swing to Houston, Jeanne's father, a law professor and philosopher, engaged in a mental game he'd enjoyed with the older kids from time to time. He asked Joseph, essentially, if he could prove his existence. Joseph recently recalled the conversation for me. His grandfather asked, "You know your reflection, how it imitates everything you do? What if it wasn't imitating you? What if you were imitating whatever that reflection did?"

Joseph said that he'd answered, "That's not true—I do stuff, and the reflection reacts." But his grandfather pressed the point. "But what if it's your *reflection's* decision, and you're just thinking, 'All right, I've got to do that now.'"

To Joseph, it was more than a brainteaser. "It was really very disturbing," he said. "He was looking for a rational debate, because he knew I was intelligent. What he didn't know was that I wasn't rational enough to argue with him." He told me that these days it would have been an interesting challenge, but at the time he didn't have the tools for debate or the emotional resilience to shrug it off.

So he went off by himself. "I stood in front of the mirror for a long time," he said.

Back in the Northeast after the vacation, Joseph told us he was hearing voices. He confided in us that the voices were those of the Greek gods, straight out of his book of *D'Aulaires' Book of Greek Myths.* And they were telling him he was a failure.

This left us panicked. Hearing voices—what researchers call "vivid auditory hallucinations"—is commonly linked to schizophrenia. What we did not know, and would not learn until we did later reading, is the growing body of work that suggests that hearing voices can be triggered[20] by childhood trauma, feelings of vulnerability, and bullying.[21]

Increasingly, Joseph was getting into trouble with other kids, but the situations weren't simple. One day the recess aides hauled him into the principal's office for throwing rocks at the other children. He admitted having thrown rocks but argued that he was only responding to their having thrown rocks at him. The principal called the others in and they admitted to having started the fight. The incident left us asking why the aides only seemed to see trouble when Joseph was causing it.

The sense that he was being accused on all sides was getting to Joseph. One day a boy he had frequent conflicts with falsely accused Joseph of poking him with a pencil. Mr. Fourth, automatically believing the other boy, packed Joseph off to the office, but not before he did get a poke in. Jeanne asked, when he got home, why he had poked the other boy. Joe said he knew he'd be punished no matter what. "If I'm going to be hanged anyway, I'd rather be hanged for a crime I committed," he said.

Whatever the reason for Joseph's decline, we knew that it was time to see a therapist again—both to help Joseph and to show the school that we were acting on their concerns. In January, we started him with a good-hearted man with a reputation for helping kids with behavioral issues get a handle on their responses. Jeanne, who had stayed home to wrangle the kids, took a half-time job at Target to help pay for the sessions; our insurance limitations on mental health care left thousands of dollars for us to pay by the end of the year.

Joe and the therapist got along well, and the therapist went a long way toward calming him down, teaching him techniques for moderating his anger. The therapist helped Joseph to understand that if his emotions were getting the best of him, he should try to remove himself from the situation. Joseph had discovered that once he got away from whatever was making him angry, the inner turmoil would evaporate almost instantly. He told Jeanne that the doctor was "the first person that year who really liked me."

In sessions without Joseph in the room, we asked whether he might talk to Joseph about his sexual orientation, to try to draw him out and help relieve some of the pressure he appeared to be under because of it. He declined, saying he would not be able to discuss such a sensitive topic until our boy was ready to bring it up himself. He said that he approved of our having given Joseph free access to the Internet, which allowed him to explore on his own and which showed him that he was not alone.

With the new therapy relationship in place, Jeanne reached out to the principal to try to explain what we felt were some of the struggles Joseph was dealing with. "I have a concern that I wanted to communicate to you about Joseph in strictest confidentiality," she wrote. She described our growing conviction that Joseph is gay, though experience had taught us not to state it in absolute terms. "I don't think it explains all of his behavior, but if true, it does explain why he is so different." And, she said, "I think people react to this on a subliminal level, kids and teachers."

The principal's e-mailed response was disappointing; he treated the letter as if Jeanne had divulged something shameful. "I know this is not an easy communication for you," he wrote.

And then he gobsmacked us with an attachment to the e-mail: a separate letter to us that had been drawn up some days before, and which suggested he was laying the groundwork for removing Joseph from the school.

> *We are especially concerned with Joseph's safety and welfare, as well as that of his classmates. Joseph's conversations with [Mr. Fourth] regarding "messages in his brain, which he can't control" and "messages he can't share because they would get him expelled from school," in view of the school district's zero tolerance policy for violent behavior, are of very serious concern. Frankly, when I aggregate all of the concerns with which Joseph is presenting us, I am becoming* <u>*alarmed*</u>*.*

Of course Joseph was troubled. But a safety risk? We showed the letter to the therapist, who scoffed at the notion that Joseph was a threat to himself or others—the standard the school would use to expel him. He needed help and treatment, the therapist said, but that's what the sessions were about, and Joseph was responding well to them. We described the kinds of actions that the teacher and principal had described to us: the pencil-pointing incident and a couple of instances of poking other kids with pencils without breaking the skin, as well as others like the moment in class when Joseph swung a book and stopped it before hitting another child. The principal was treating these incidents the same as if Joseph had brought a switchblade to class instead of school supplies, explaining, essentially, that a pencil in his hands could be a weapon in the legal sense of the word.

The therapist heard us out and said, "This seems an extreme threat for this kind of behavior." The therapist further observed that the school seemed to misinterpret Joseph's behavior as defiant. Nor was this being seen as simple contrariness, but as a pathological condition known as oppositional defiant disorder. Children with ODD fight authority figures for the sake of fighting, and lash out at their peers to harass and annoy and to get attention. With the school, as with the coach, the lens used to view the behavior mattered. The therapist said it was vital to clear things up with the school: to explain that Joseph might be acting out of frustration and controlling it poorly but that he was not engaging in intentional defiance. He said the school needed to understand that Joseph would respond well to the cognitive behavioral therapy and anger management techniques he would receive over the course of therapy, and so there was no need for expulsion.

Until then, we had thought of the principal as well intended but out of his depth. Now we wondered if he was using loaded language and thinly veiled diagnoses to rid himself of a problem. Jeanne started looking into private schools in our area, and soon realized that we couldn't afford them. The mother of the other scapegoated boy in the class—who actually got tougher treatment than Joseph from Mr. Fourth—would move to Florida at the end of the school year. But we were tied to the town; our other two children were settled into the middle school and the high school.

Jeanne and I felt trapped. The tension and anger was leaking into every part of our lives, our stomachs knotted through the day as we waited for the phone to ring with the latest problem. Jeanne was having trouble sleeping and recalled her shifts at Target passing in a daze. "It was as if I was drowning," she says.

One day at Target, a customer put a big, ceramic cookie jar on the conveyor belt; it was brown and tan, and its sides were slick. "My mind had just drifted away," Jeanne says, "and when I came back to myself, I had dropped the jar on the floor and it smashed." She thought, *I really need to get a grip. Literally.*

The psychologist became an advocate for Joseph with the school, recommending that teachers try to deal with him in a less confrontational way. He told us, too, that "Joseph has to understand his contribution" to the problem. "We have to give him a message that this kind of behavior is unacceptable."

He also suggested some new rules. The school allowed Joseph to leave Mr. Fourth's classroom when things began to get heated and go across the hall to the speech therapist's office and calm himself down. And for a while, the teacher told me he was making an effort to get into fewer fights with him, and told me "I do see improvements in how he is responding to things."

But, in fact, the teacher was deteriorating. He was disorganized, and his teaching had become increasingly slapdash. He would go over a new topic lightly—say, long division—and then blow up at the class when the failing grades came back. The teacher became more and more critical of individual kids aside from Joseph as well, focusing on their shortcomings in front of the entire class and humiliating them.

The broadened focus didn't take the pressure off Joseph.

Instead, it inflamed his sense of injustice. He battled Mr. Fourth over his treatment of another boy in the class. We called it "putting on his Captain America tights" and tried to tell him that he didn't have to fight everyone else's fights.

Even today, Joseph remembers some of the disputes vividly, especially the ones about politics. In those early years after the 9/11 attacks, Mr. Fourth saw it as his duty to teach the children patriotism and the evils of Islamic fundamentalism. There was no mention in his freewheeling lectures of the growing criticism of the attack on Iraq, or the soundness of the evidence put forth by the Bush administration to justify the invasion—topics that were much discussed at our dinner table.

One day, Joseph recalled, the teacher was engaging in full-blown Islamophobia, speaking of terrorism as if it were a solely Muslim phenomenon.

Joseph raised his hand and confronted the teacher about the sweeping statement. "There are white terrorists," he said.

"Name one group!" Mr. Fourth responded hotly.

"What about the Michigan Militia?" Joseph retorted.

"Prove it," the teacher huffed.

That was Joseph's flypaper mind at work. The Michigan Militia was a paramilitary group that had been linked to extremists, and had been immortalized in a 1997 song by Moxy Frúvous, a left-leaning Toronto band we loved and whose CDs we often played in the car. Joseph, always asking questions, had wanted to know what the song was about, which had led to discussions of extremists, Timothy McVeigh and the Oklahoma City bombing, and other examples of homegrown American terrorism.

We weren't happy with the escalating conflict in the classroom.

But we also understood what Joseph was angry about: the politicization of his school and the prejudice his teacher was trying to indoctrinate the impressionable children under his care with. I love my country and will stand my own patriotism up against anyone else's. But it's a patriotism built on the free exchange of ideas, not propaganda. And Joe is my son.

In mid-March, Mr. Fourth called me at work. "Unfortunately, this is not a pleasant call," he said. "He kind of pushed me over the edge today."

The confrontation had started when another child told him that Joseph had gotten so upset that he was banging his head against the back of a chair. "I didn't have a clue as to why that happened," the teacher said.

Joseph, he said, insulted him in front of the other students, calling him a "mindless old bag who runs this classroom like a prison."

The teacher told me it was "more than I should have to put up with." He complained that "he was so defiant, and so abusive and arrogant today," and said, "I honestly don't know how to break him of it."

I told him that we would talk to Joseph. I was too unsettled by the call to say what I wanted most desperately to say: Why are you trying to "break" my child? And I couldn't help but wonder what I thought whenever I saw parents warring with their kids: somebody's got to be the grown-up here.

At the end of March, the worst blowup occurred. It had started when Joseph talked back to the teacher in class, once again enraging him. (According to the principal's postmortem, Joseph had been making jokes and the teacher had said the class didn't need a class clown. Joseph responded, "That's funny, because it's got so many of them.")

The two of them began yelling at each other. The teacher set up a chair in the hallway, just outside the door of the classroom, and told him to sit there. Joseph headed across the hall to the speech therapist—but this time, she wasn't in her office. He went to the classroom of a friendly teacher along the same hallway to sit and calm himself down. But his teacher stormed into one classroom after another until he found Joseph and dragged him back to the punishment chair.

Joseph came home more distraught than we had seen him in months.

I wrote to the principal and said that this had to stop. I pointed to steps we had taken to improve the situation, and asked again that Joseph be switched to another teacher. The principal responded:

> *I appreciate your insights and continuing cooperation. I can assure you that we will continue to do our best for Joseph and will do our best to resolve the "interesting challenges" he is posing. Fortunately, Joseph's classmates are very tolerant and compassionate, and although he sometimes appears intense, [Mr. Fourth] is committed to doing what's best for Joseph. I know the challenges for both you at home and us at school can sometimes be frustrating, but I'm confident we can cooperatively endure and we both have Joseph's best interests as our priority.*
>
> *I have considered your idea regarding a change of teacher for Joseph. There are a number of reasons why*

> *I cannot support this. When we meet I can share some
> of the reasons with you. (Suffice it to say for now that
> we have some interesting "challenges" in other class-
> rooms as well as in [Mr. Fourth's], including the class-
> room you mentioned in a previous correspondence.)*

He closed by defending the teacher and urging us to get his
side of any incident, saying that the teacher "continues to go
well 'above and beyond' to respond to Joseph."

Jeanne and I were growing desperate and no help was coming from the school administration. But the rest of the staff did
its best to back Joseph up. When the speech therapist would
hear Mr. Fourth start to yell at Joseph, she would make a quiet
call to the office. The office would then ring the intercom in
Joseph's classroom to ask that Joseph be sent to the nurse before
things got too far out of hand.

I spoke with the speech therapist again while working on
this book, and she said she was still angry about the treatment
that Joseph got at the hands of Mr. Fourth. She had fallen for
Joseph the day he used the word "ethnocentric" in conversation
with her. And while she had concerns about his deteriorating
emotional state that year, she thought most of his problems
would have been solved by getting him away from Mr. Fourth.

"Power," she said, "has no place in the classroom."

One day in March, Jeanne called me at work. Had I approved
a battery of tests for Joseph? He had come home chattering
about how much fun he was having with the exercises. I hadn't;
the school had decided to evaluate him for disabilities as a step
toward classification.

As part of that process, the school sent us to a psychiatrist affiliated with the district to evaluate Joseph. The school's goal was to resolve their question of whether he was a threat to himself or other students. It would also help them to prepare for something called an Individual Education Plan.

We were struggling to learn the jargon of federal and state education rules; the IEP, as it is known, would serve as a contract between us and the school to set the conditions for the way the school treated him. A social worker on the staff called to allay our fears and our confusion; the point of the IEP process, she said, was to help Joseph, not to judge him or expel him. "We're not dying to put kids out," she said.

Joseph and I drove to the psychiatrist's office on a stunningly beautiful spring day. I tried to prepare him, to tell him not to be intimidated. I said that if he could not get angry when talking about his teacher, that would help.

"Don't worry," he said to me. "I know exactly what to say to these people."

I don't know what he thought that meant, but once he walked in, he chattered blithely about hearing voices and his conviction that the other children were arrayed against him. He also explained to the doctor that he had a secret, but "if I told you, I would have to kill you."

I held my breath waiting for the report to arrive. But when it did, it was as close to vindication as we could hope for. The doctor saw a troubled boy with "mental distortions," but not a boy who was a threat. He wrote approvingly of the psychotherapy Joseph was receiving and said it should continue; he did not recommend a regimen of medication.

Everything seemed to be moving toward the IEP meeting,

which I could not help but see as a showdown. By mid-April the testing was complete. The school's social worker said that one test was performed "to see the ceiling on his reading, but the test didn't go high enough." The overall results showed none of the deep-seated learning disabilities that some of his teachers had claimed, but "we definitely see the emotional piece," she said. It was true, she acknowledged, that the relationship with the teacher was not "the best fit in the world" for Joseph, but she said he was presenting challenges as well. "There are things he brings to the table that are unique to Joseph." Under the demands and pressures of school, she said, "I do see a different Joseph at school than you see at home."

The speech therapist and some of her colleagues were Joseph's amen corner. "We are 100 percent behind Joseph," she said.

The day of the meeting came. The teacher gave his presentation describing Joseph's behavior and told the story of Joseph pointing the pencil at him. He talked about the couple of incidents when Joseph poked other children with a pencil. In this room, with the rest of the child study team listening for signs of a serious threat, his words sounded hollow. He spoke for a while but soon wound down, uncertainly.

Next, the results of the testing were described. The reports showed no evidence of classic autism symptoms or ADHD, and even observed that he was "persistent in his work" and did not flinch when the testing coordinator rested her hand on his shoulder to guide him back to class.

The coordinator for gifted and talented programs for the school district had expressed an interest in getting Joseph involved in programs that would present him with the kinds of intellectual challenges that could help him develop to his potential, while dealing with the apparent learning disability that had shown up in the testing that made it so hard for him to write his work. There is, of course, an abbreviation for this: GT/LD, for "gifted and talented/learning disabled."

It was my turn to talk. What Joseph needed, I said, was to be treated with the blend of firmness and compassion that the substitute teacher at the beginning of the year had proven to be so effective. I explained that several teachers over the years had offered their informal diagnoses and suggested we look into medications for Joseph. I explained our view that we were reluctant to give medications to a child so young unless we were sure that his condition required it and that the medications would help. I pointed out that the one professional qualified to prescribe drugs, the psychiatrist, had not seen the dire threat that the teacher claimed to have seen. I read off the side effects of the drugs that are commonly prescribed for the conditions that teachers over time had suggested Joseph had. One of them, Risperdal, which is prescribed for psychosis, has side effects that include weight gain. And diabetes. And anhedonia, or a loss of joy in life. The room got very, very quiet.

The meeting ended with an agreement that Joseph's accommodations would be focused on behavioral issues, with special emphasis on constructive criticism and a lack of direct confrontation. There would be extra time on tests. Other accommodations included the right to leave the classroom for one of his safe places when under stress without being followed out. The punishment chair was not an option. There would be weekly meetings with the school psychologist.

As the year wound to a close, Joseph's mood lightened. His

subconscious seemed to be easing up, too. Earlier in that awful school year, Joseph came downstairs one morning and told Jeanne about a harrowing dream. She told me, "Joseph was on an island with a bunch of kids," and the teacher "was killing one a day. He knew that it would be his turn soon."

By the end of that year, some of the pressures had receded. He stopped talking about the secret. Jeanne asked him whether it was still bothering him; without saying explicitly what the agitation had been about, he told her that he had talked to other kids and they did the same kind of thing he did. We took it to mean that once he found out that other kids his age were looking at naughty bits online, he relaxed—even if the naughty bits he was looking at weren't the same ones that fascinated the other kids.

The most important thing was this: the school year ended. We had survived. In the dwindling days of the semester, I dropped by the school for the final assembly. These events were always packed, so I walked up to the balcony and saw the fourth-grade teacher. He smiled and motioned me over. I sat down next to him and asked a question that had eaten at me for months. "Why did you even teach this year?" I asked. "You were in such pain!"

He replied, "I wish I hadn't had to, Mr. Schwartz." He explained that under the state system, his disability payments would have been minuscule. "I couldn't live on what they would have paid me."

For our part, we were simply relieved to be done with Mr. Fourth. But he wasn't done with his scapegoats. The following year, a neighbor sought me out. His son, who had never had problems at school, had been singled out for criticism and was taking it very badly. The crossing guard, remembering Joseph's troubles with the same teacher, suggested that the father speak with me. The father was bewildered by Mr. Fourth's accusations about the boy. Among other things, the teacher had accused him of "rolling and crawling around on the floor," something the father had never seen him do at home or at church.

Something had changed, however. This time, when the family took their complaints to the principal at the end of the school year—and handed over an ill-advised letter the teacher had written to the family with comments that could be construed as racist—the principal told them that he would work to make sure that this didn't happen again. The year after that, the teacher retired.

I recently spoke with Joseph's third-grade teacher, who talked about her recommendation that he be put in Mr. Fourth's class.

"I've always felt guilty about that," she said.

CHAPTER SIX

By this time, we were confident that Joseph's sexual orientation was gay, and that that seemed to be causing him a range of problems and pressures despite our efforts at school and the loving support he had at home. But there were other things going on with him that no one had precisely put a finger on. At the end of fourth grade, he was clearly having problems with mental illness. Like many other families, we had relatives with a history of depression. But while a family history of depression is considered a risk factor, it was imposible to determine its effect. We didn't know whether or not Joseph was mentally ill and gay, or possibly mentally ill in part because he was gay. We had to figure out whether he was driven into mental illness because of stress, as we strongly suspected, or whether this was our new reality. Would he hear voices forever, or would he get better?

In the broader context of American life, mental illness is not so unusual. Many of us have some kind of additional element of mental strain that complicates our lives, though the exact prevalence is a matter of some dispute.

The first nationally representative study to determine the prevalence of mental disorders among Americans was the federally funded National Comorbidity Survey,[22] which began in 1990 and has been updated[23] in the years since. These studies identified mental illness by using the definitions in the Diagnostic and Statistical Manual of Mental Disorders (DSM). The numbers that resulted are surprising: one-quarter of those studied had experienced some form of a mental disorder in the previous twelve months. Nearly half of those surveyed had at least one disorder during their lifetime.[24]

That high estimate is controversial among scientists, and many say it's an inflated product of overly broad definitions. Jerome Wakefield, professor of social work and psychiatry at New York University, told the *Wall Street Journal* in 2011 that many of the people reporting symptoms of mental illness, and especially depression, might be experiencing a normal reaction to abnormal events, such as depression over losing a job. "We have had so much trouble distinguishing disorder from stress and eccentricity," he said.[25] Government statistics on serious mental illness from the National Institute of Mental Health suggest that the incidence of conditions profound enough to cause disability is much smaller: a bit less than 5 percent in the overall population.[26]

Dr. Wakefield is not opposed to psychiatry for those with what he calls "harmful dysfunction," but he has suggested that there is more than a little self-interest for the mental health and medical professions in what he calls the "medicalization of sadness."[27] In an essay he cowrote with Allan V. Horwitz, a professor of sociology at Rutgers University, they noted that "millions of people now seek professional help for conditions that fall under the medicalized, overly inclusive definition of depression," and "the medicalization of depression has proven to be even more profitable for pharmaceutical companies, whose sales of anti-depressant medications have soared." Many of those people experiencing "normal sadness" might find that it goes away over time, they wrote.[28] In their 2007 book, *The Loss of Sadness: How Psychiatry Transformed Normal Sorrow into Depressive Disorder*, Dr. Horwitz and Dr. Wakefield refer to the "enticements by insurance reimbursement to see depressive disorder whenever possible."[29]

Diagnoses of psychological issues are relatively common among youngsters, as well. For children eight to fifteen years of age, according to figures from the U.S. Centers for Disease Control and Prevention, the prevalence of "any disorder" in the previous twelve months is more than 13 percent, with nearly 9 percent having ADHD and 3.7 percent having "mood disorders." Major depression afflicted 2.7 percent, and 0.7 percent had anxiety disorders.[30]

Any way you look at it there's a lot of mental affliction out there.

Against that background level of psychological problems, there is another factor for parents of gay kids to consider: homosexuality has been associated with greater incidence of mental illness than the general population. It's important to consider the reasons for this, and to understand the long and controversial path to the current way that most experts think about it. The tendency to jump to conclusions about the correlation has led to a long historical wrangle over what it all means.

It wasn't so long ago that homosexuality itself was considered a form of mental illness. The American Psychiatric Association's first DSM, published in 1952, listed homosexuality as one of the "sexual deviations" that fell under the broad heading of "sociopathic personality disturbance."[31]

The passage seemed to have less to do with scientific evidence than with attitudes as old as the text of Leviticus: "Do not lie with a male as one lies with a woman; it is an abhorrence." In fact, the harsh diagnostic assessment in the first DSM was a McCarthy-era departure from an earlier, more accepting view of homosexuality from the father of psychiatry himself. Sigmund Freud wrote a letter in 1935 to an American mother worried about her son:

> Homosexuality is assuredly no advantage, but it is nothing to be ashamed of, no vice, no degradation, it cannot be classified as an illness; we consider it to be a variation of the sexual function produced by a certain arrest of sexual development. Many highly respectable individuals of ancient and modern times have been homosexuals, several of the greatest men among them (Plato, Michelangelo, Leonardo da Vinci, etc.). It is a great injustice to persecute homosexuality as a crime, and cruelty too. . . .

As for her request to treat her son, he wrote that if she wanted to rid him of homosexuality, the chances of success were poor: "In a general way we cannot promise to achieve it." If the son "is unhappy, neurotic, torn by conflicts, inhibited in his social life, analysis may bring him harmony, peace of mind, full efficiency whether he remains a homosexual or gets changed."[32]

The fact that the psychiatric community would declare homosexuality to be a "sociopathic personality disturbance" just seventeen years later shows that the question of mental health and homosexuality has undergone a series of pendulum swings over time.

When science came around to study the matter without the blinders of morality, it put the DSM classification in doubt. Dr. Evelyn Hooker published the landmark study in the field in 1957. Until then, the usual course of research on homosexuals involved studying people who had sought psychological treatment. That made them easy to find, but those subjects were more likely to have problems than the general population, a phenomenon known as selection bias. So Dr. Hooker administered a battery of well-established psychological tests to a group of homosexual and heterosexual men who were not seeking psychotherapy. She then had experts review the tests without knowing the sexual orientation of the men. Her panel found no significant differences between the psychological health of gay and straight subjects. Dr. Hooker concluded "homosexuality as a clinical entity does not exist,"[33] and over decades, further research confirmed and expanded on those conclusions. She found nothing inherent in homosexuality itself that caused, or was caused by, mental illness.

Twenty-one years after the first DSM's diagnosis, the American Psychiatric Association voted to support Hooker's view, and removed homosexuality from the second edition of the manual. The controversy was not over, however, because a faction within the psychiatric community that believed homosexuality is a treatable illness—conservative doctors like Charles Socarides, who pioneered so-called reparative therapies—continued to try to swing the pendulum back again. Their argument that liberal therapists had monkeyed with the DSM became part of the conservative argument that pro-gay activists were pursuing a "homosexual agenda." Any possible link between homosexuality and mental illness was now firmly a part of a broader culture war, not just scholarly disagreement.

That counter-pressure contributed to the inclusion of a new condition, "ego-dystonic homosexuality," in the third edition of the DSM in 1980; the term described people who were deeply distressed by their sexual orientation. By 1986, the pendulum would swing once again and the diagnosis was removed. As Ilan Meyer of UCLA put it in a 2007 paper that laid out some of the history, the wariness among "gay-affirmative" psychiatrists and psychologists about suggesting that homosexuality is a disorder may have led them to interpret research findings in a way that understated the prevalence of mental distress or disorder.[34]

While the controversy continued, a new wave of social science research sought a different path. These researchers acknowledged that a higher prevalence of mental health problems were correlated with homosexuality, but found new reasons to explain the relationship, suggesting that external pressures, not anything inherent in homosexuality, were the cause. This more subtle view—that being gay might be correlated with problems like substance abuse, depression, and anxiety, without actually being caused by it—got a push in the

1990s. That was partly because of the emerging AIDS epidemic, but in a broader way, said social scientists Susan D. Cochran and Vickie M. Mays. In a 2006 paper, they wrote that the new approach reflected a rising trend in research to find "the possible harmful effects of social inequality due to social status, including ethnicity, race, gender, and social class."[35] And those studies would show that gay men and lesbians did, in fact, have a somewhat higher prevalence of mental disorders and suicide than their heterosexual counterparts. But there is nothing unique to gays or lesbians in such a conclusion, they explained: the pressures that can result from being gay could contribute to the kinds of problems that similar pressures would cause anyone to experience. Gregory Herek of University of California, Davis, who has studied the effects of prejudice against sexual minorities, summed up the Cochran and Mays research this way on a Web page he has created regarding the issues of mental health and homosexuality:[36] "The data from some studies suggest that, although most sexual minority individuals are well adjusted, nonheterosexuals may be at somewhat heightened risk for depression, anxiety, and related problems, compared to exclusive heterosexuals."

Herek wrote, "Indeed, given the stresses created by sexual stigma and prejudice, it would be surprising if some of them did not manifest psychological problems."

Are there other conditions potentially linked to homosexuality as well? In our own family's experience, teachers and some of the doctors we encountered suggested Joseph might have an autism spectrum disorder. We did not think this was the case, as I've said. But a friend at work, the parent of a kid on the spectrum, told me that she had heard about research that suggested a link between homosexuality and Asperger's.

It was a startling idea—I hadn't heard it before. And it sent me digging.

Certainly, spectrum disorders are surprisingly common, especially in boys. The Centers for Disease Control estimated in 2012 that 1 in 88 children has an autism spectrum disorder to some degree. Boys are nearly five times more likely to get a diagnosis of one of the disorders.[37] More conservative estimates published by the National Institutes of Health put the incidence closer to 1 in 1,000.[38]

While there is a long history of research into the LGBT population and mental disorders like depression as the rest of this chapter shows, I had no luck finding studies that discussed any association between being gay and spectrum disorders.

To see whether I had missed something, I called Steve Silberman. He's done decades of groundbreaking science journalism in *Wired* magazine and other publications, and is in the middle of a book project himself on autism and neurodiversity. If anyone had seen such research, it would be Steve.

When I called him, he sighed. While he, too, had heard much anecdotal discussion of such a link, "there's no support in the research world," he said; "People aren't doing that kind of research yet."

Anecdotes aren't proof, and as of now, there's no evidence to support an autism-gay link. The astronomer Carl Sagan popularized an important rule of science. "Extraordinary claims require extraordinary evidence." Whatever others might have thought, there was no evidence to show that Joe, or any child, was more likely to be on the autism spectrum because he is gay.

The other mental issues we've discussed, however—such as depression, anxiety, and substance abuse—are more prevalent in the lesbian and gay population than in the heterosexual population. Explaining how that happens has been the work of researchers like Ilan Meyer, who has promoted the idea of "minority stress." It's a complex interaction of factors. Dr. Meyer has written many papers to describe the phenomenon, but it all came alive in a San Francisco courtroom in 2010 when he testified as an expert witness in the lawsuit over California's Proposition 8, the 2008 voter initiative that banned same-sex marriage. The plaintiffs, who want to overturn Proposition 8, called Dr. Meyer as a friendly witness to show that by treating same-sex couples differently—barring them from marrying as heterosexual couples do—society perpetuates a cycle of unhappiness and stress.

Dr. Meyer's testimony was a masterful synthesis of hundreds, perhaps thousands, of scientific papers and articles—a sobering distillation of the interconnected ways that stress builds in the minds and lives of gay people, and the effects that it can have.

Under questioning on the stand, Dr. Meyer identified four types of minority stress. The first type are incidents that he called "prejudice events." These could be something as horrifying as a beating or seemingly minor "everyday discrimination event." Those lesser "daily hassles," he said, could be as simple as having to deal with administrative forms that call for marital status. Under Proposition 8, he said, a gay person, even someone in a domestic partnership might look at the form and sigh, "There is no place for me to put anything here." These seemingly small insults add up, he said, and "what it means is social rejection," echoing larger incidents of rejection and disrespect from the past.

The second type of minority stress, he said, is the expectation of rejection and discrimination. Dr. Meyer described it in a chilling way: as feelings commonly experienced by a gay couple walking down the street. "Very often, regardless of how friendly their street is, they would have to monitor the kind of affection that they display with each other because perhaps somebody will come and throw stones and eggs, and so forth, because they bring up something the person doesn't like."

It all requires "a certain vigilance," he said; "you have to be on edge; you have to watch; you have to have a third eye, looking, monitoring your environment."

People confronting those pressures may decide that it's simply easier not to deal with the overt and subtle prejudice, and might just stay in the closet. But that, Dr. Meyer testified, introduces pressures of its own, shown over and over in studies. "There's a stress that is involved with concealing, because you have to work really hard on this." Maintaining a lie over time is stressful, as any soldier living under the "Don't Ask, Don't Tell" regime could attest. The pressure, he said, comes from "hiding something that is perceived as being such a core thing about who you are."

Gay people, he noted, often say "this is who I am" when talking about their sexuality. "That doesn't mean gay people are just that. But it is a central identity that is important. And if you want to express who you are, certainly, you wouldn't want to hide that part."

Concealment stress, he said, comes down to something fundamental: whether you are "living an authentic life."

Another way that hiding complicates a closeted gay person's life, he said, is that it cuts off the support one might get from family, friends, and community. Someone might be able to get support at a gay community center, or by marching in a pride parade "you get certain benefits from being in that environment that maybe you don't get in other places."

But of course, "if you are concealing your gay identity, you are not going to walk into a gay community center or gay pride event." This element of minority stress, Dr. Meyer explained, divides the kind of stress experienced by gays from that expressed by racial minorities. A black child who experiences prejudice can run to his mother for comfort, or hear inspiring stories of overcoming prejudice at church; a gay child or teenager, especially one who is concealing his sexual identity, may not feel capable of seeking that support. Even if there are other gay children around, they might be concealing their sexual orientation as well, so the sense of isolation is increased.

The fourth source of minority stress, Dr. Meyer explained in the courtroom, is known in the literature as "internalized homophobia." It is the process of taking to heart society's negative attitudes about homosexuality. Dr. Meyer cited a bestseller from the 1960s, *Everything You Always Wanted to Know About Sex* But Were Afraid to Ask,* by David Reuben.

Earlier in his testimony, Dr. Meyer read a passage from the book's breezy question-and-answer text aloud in court to describe the social stigma society places on gay people:

> *"What about all the homosexuals who live together happily for years?"*
>
> *And the answer is: "What about them? They are mighty rare birds among the homosexual flock.*

Moreover, the 'happy' part remains to be seen. The bitterest argument between a husband and wife is a passionate love sonnet by comparison with a dialogue between a butch and his queen. Live together? Yes. Happily? Hardly."

Now, in talking about internalized homophobia, he came back to that passage. If someone who had read the Reuben book begins to recognize same-sex attraction, he is likely to think, "Everything that I've learned about what it is to be gay, that must be what I am." Something like that passage from *Everything You Always Wanted to Know About Sex*, will be quite devastating," he explained, "if they believe that and thought, Well, this is what is in my future."

These anguished feelings, he said, impinge upon our sense of what is known as the "possible self"—our imagined future, our mental construct of the possibilities ahead. "The possible self is not only important because of how it projects to the future and how it maybe helps a person think about the future," he explained. "It is also related to what people feel right now" about themselves.

Research bears this out, he said. "Gay and lesbian youth had a harder time projecting to the future because they have learned those kind of negative attitudes." If they can't see a future for themselves as other kids do—even something seemingly as simple as being able to marry some day—their future is likely to narrow accordingly, he said.

The interlaced effects of the four kinds of minority stress, Dr. Meyer said, can play out in harmful consequences for health: the higher incidence of depression, anxiety, and substance abuse that so many studies have shown. "There are also just what we would call general distress or just feeling something, blue and sad, things like that," he said.

Anyone who experiences stress can suffer from these disorders, he acknowledged, but "gay and lesbian populations are exposed to more of the stress and—to distress, which is unique and additive" to the stress that afflicts the general population. "That excess risk is associated with excess disease" or disorder, he explained.

And, as if to nail the point, a lawyer for those trying to overturn Proposition 8, Christopher D. Dusseault, asked Dr. Meyer, "Are you saying that being gay or lesbian is in and of itself in any way a mental illness?"

Meyer's response was simple and firm. "No, not at all," he said. But there are risks associated with stigma and prejudice, and the excess risk is related to excess disorders of many kinds.

Mr. Dusseault then read the paragraph from Healthy People 2010 that grimly stated:

America's gay and lesbian population comprises a diverse community with disparate health concerns. Major health issues for gay men are HIV/AIDS and other sexually transmitted diseases, substance abuse, depression, and suicide. Gay male adolescents are two to three times more likely than their peers to attempt suicide. Some evidence suggests lesbians have higher rates of smoking, being overweight, alcohol abuse, and stress than heterosexual women. The issues surrounding personal, family, and social acceptance of sexual

> *orientation can place a significant burden on mental*
> *health and personal safety.*

Dr. Meyer said, "I think it basically describes what I was talking about today."

Some experts argue that the stark and frightening statistics laid out in reports like Healthy People 2010 don't reflect a changing reality among today's teenagers.

The work of Ritch C. Savin-Williams, the director of the Cornell University Sex and Gender Lab, suggests another swing of the research pendulum could be under way. His research and impassioned writings claim that the political pressures that brought renewed focus to the troubles of gay adolescents have overshot the mark, and that it's time to see gay kids as, generally, just fine, thanks. He points to the fact—never denied by previous researchers—that even if the percentage of gay kids having problems is higher than the percentage of kids having problems in the general population, the majority are not having those problems.

In his 2005 book, *The New Gay Teenager (Adolescent Lives)*, Professor Savin-Williams wrote that the research suffered from the same selection bias that afflicted earlier work: that the study population was dominated by adolescents with problems, like a study that included a number of Seattle street hustlers, and later studies that examined the problems of kids who had sought counseling and crisis intervention. "Being gay, young, and *troubled* had thus been intrinsically, even purposefully linked. The linkage made grant proposals and justifications for increased educational and mental-health services an easier sell," he wrote.

By comparison, in his own experience with gay teens from the mid-1980s onward, Professor Savin-Williams found them in general to be refreshingly untroubled. "Maybe they were healthy. Maybe we adults were wrong," he wrote. [39]

When I called Dr. Savin-Williams to ask about his research, he told me, "I think some of the healthiest students I know are gay."

He characterized the earlier work on the psychological problems of gay teens as "doom and gloom" research, but added, "I never want to attack the good people who were doing the research—they were trying to identify a population that really needed some help," he said. "In a real way, they accomplished that—they were able to get resources like gay-straight alliances, and a sort of sensitivity to the plight of gay youth."

Yes, there are some gay kids who are troubled, he said, but "there are overweight kids who are very troubled. There are some unattractive girls who are very troubled. The ultimate question is, 'are there more gay youth that are troubled than straight youth?' I believe that's *not* true," he said. "Though there's a mountain of evidence, seemingly scientific evidence, against my point of view."

He recognizes that most experts disagree with him, but insists that "if you look at the evidence critically, it does not support the doom and gloom point of view."

Savin-Williams's approach seems to downplay the problems that emerge in places that are not tolerant, and the torment of kids who do have problems. Some experts believe that he selectively interprets the data to support a philosophical position. Alice Dreger, the bioethicist at Northwestern University, put it this way in an e-mail about his work: "Ritch is determined to prove that gay youth would be *totally fine* in the right environment, but that seems to me a tautology sometimes." The right environment would be a society that's completely accepting of homosexuality, and that's still not the world we live in, she said. "We have to live in the real world and worry about real kids."

In our case, kids like Joe.

CHAPTER SEVEN

Most people are basically evenly balanced. They are not demons, pious knights, or any other similar creature. The saintly enjoy being pious. The devilish enjoy being evil. The average person is fanatical to neither cause. But there is a fragment of evil in a saint, and a spark of good in a devil. No one is completely good or evil, no one completely balanced.

—JOSEPH SCHWARTZ, AGE TEN

We were driving from Michigan to New Jersey. We had dropped Elizabeth off at college and were heading back along the endlessness of Interstate 80. Joe, in the backseat, asked if he could use my laptop. So I slipped it out of my backpack and handed it to him, and he started typing. And typing. And typing.

By the time we got home, he had finished a short story that began, "Once upon a time, in a land called Kasse, there was an evil queen who was enslaving all the townsfolk. (Yeah, yeah, I know, standard fairy-tale rhetoric. But it gets better.)"

Joe had picked out a black-letter font for the story, evoking the dark, mythic mood, and he laid out the narrative with his usual knowing wink. When he finished that story, he moved on to write a brief essay, a meditation on the blend of good and evil in the human mind. That essay, quoted above, ended with: "You may say that I lie, you may say that I have lost my mind, but you know that these are not the ravings of the insane. You know this in your heart." Whatever else might be going on in his life, a sharp and creative Joseph was still there, tapping away at the keys.

We had approached fifth grade fretfully. After the awful year we'd had with the bullying Mr. Fourth, Joe was scared of his own shadow. Jeanne and I weren't much better off.

But the therapist had said something very important to us: "You're driving the train. You're in charge." Joe was our child. It was up to us to tell the school how to help us. It was up to us to protect him, to work with the school to set the rules and make sure the school followed them. It was up to us whether or not he was prescribed medication. "You're driving the train" would become one of the phrases that stayed with us, guided us.

So over the summer, Jeanne sat down at her computer and started typing a note to the fifth-grade teacher. By the time she was finished, it was six single-spaced pages long—nearly three thousand words. We worked on it together, creating what we would eventually call "the Joseph manual," and ran it by the therapist for his additions and tweaks. It began with what we hoped would come across as cheery honesty:

With the new school year beginning, we are looking forward to a fresh start. We wanted to share with you

what we've learned in the last few years about Joseph,
who is both a bright kid and a handful.

We wrote that Joseph "is working hard on developing the emotional maturity to keep him from overreacting to teasing and to classroom conflict," and that with the new IEP in place to help guide the school in how to deal with him, "we believe that things will improve." We laid out Joe's psychological evaluation from the previous year and described the uncanny range of topics he could expound on, from King Baldwin of Jerusalem to minor figures in Greek mythology. ("Whenever we have a question or are confused about something, we always turn to Joseph to see if he knows the answer," we wrote.) The note explained the odd "gifted and talented/learning disability" label, and put a lot of effort into explaining that although his behavior in class might seem like ADHD or Asperger's, the testing performed by the school had not suggested that he had either condition.

The point of the note, we wrote, was that it would suggest techniques the teacher could use "to get the best out of Joe." Those techniques, backed up by the therapist's recommendations and the terms of the Individual Education Plan, included "consistent and predictable" teaching methods and classroom environment, with no yelling. Constructive criticism, please, not negative comments. And please do what you can to keep the other kids from teasing him.

If Joe gets upset in class, we explained, he might bite the back of his hand, pace the room, or not do his class work. Giving him a minute or two to calm himself down, we explained, can be remarkably effective. We noted that we weren't worried about the biting, since it helped Joe settle himself and did not actually hurt him. If the behavior isn't disruptive, "please try to ignore it." If any of the behaviors must be corrected, gentle and calm is the way to go. "Confrontation will only make him more anxious," we wrote. "This behavior and the feelings of stress that cause it are being taken very seriously and are the center-piece of his ongoing therapy."

And so, "We are not saying that Joseph should never be subjected to any discipline, only that it has to be imposed in a firm, but fair, way."

We are working with the therapist to help Joseph develop a thicker skin, but for now it is best to avoid all of these situations. Rather than get into a confrontation over uncompleted work, please just send it home and we will make sure it gets done. One of the characteristics of Joseph's learning disability the testing uncovered was a difficulty performing on command under a time deadline. Please remember that this is a learning disability, not simple defiance or laziness.

With a few more tips and a request, also based on the IEP, that Joseph be given a computer keyboard to work with, we ended the note hoping for the best.

As we were finishing up the manual, Jeanne sent me an e-mail at work to say that she had edited it one more time before sending, she said, to "cut out a little of the niceness." Being accommodating and friendly is great, she wrote, but "I wanted it clear that if they dared to put Joseph in a chair in the hallway, there would be consequences this time. They have the test scores and the classification now, they goddamn well better not try that shit again."

With smiles on our faces and steel in our spines, we moved forward. I called the fifth-grade teacher just before classes started to make sure that he had received our note, and to find out if he had any questions. To my relief, he opened the conversation by saying "a lot of the things you have written down here are things I agree with wholeheartedly." There would be no problem with Joe using a computer, and "I would not accept any negative peer behaviors," he said. He was beginning his thirty-third year of teaching, having missed just ten days of school in that time. "Five days for the birth of each child," he said. He asked for any background material we had on GT/LD kids.

The teacher had a good sense of humor, and he and Joseph clicked. Joseph's behavior in class began to improve over the previous year's almost immediately. With no teacher yelling at him, Joseph wasn't yelling back, wasn't hiding in the closet, wasn't biting his hand or getting into fights with the other kids. The calls to the house stopped, along with the trips to the principal. He performed well: when the kids in the school took a statewide writing exam, the graders called the school to make sure that Joseph's test hadn't been filled in by an adult.

Looking back, Joe called the year as a happy one, with academic challenges that he dove into. For one assignment, the kids were reading a book that had animals for characters. The book included a wedding attended by animals of many species. "Write up a menu for the wedding," the teacher said, "that caters to any animals that might attend." As Joseph tells it, "I went all out," spending hours at the keyboard in a resource room writing up delicacies for horses, geese, bunnies, "and innumerable small, furry animals." Inspired in part by the feasts described by Brian Jacques in the Redwall series, Joe imagined dandelion salad for the bunnies, roasted oats and vanilla-infused apples for the horses, and more.

Joseph recalled with pride that as he worked away, the aide in the resource room looked over his shoulder at one point and said, "Oh, my God, that looks delicious—and I'm not even a horse."

Throughout that year, however, some tensions remained. There was a special education aide in the classroom to monitor Joseph's behavior; this was against the therapist's instructions, but the teacher had demanded an aide in case Joseph blew up. The aide's attempts to help him do his math irritated him. Joseph has always been good at math and wanted to be treated like the other kids. His occasional flare-ups of temper had to do with the interference. It was nothing enormous, but it was enough to remind us that not everything was perfect.

Aside from that kind of nagging problem, things were so much better that our feeling of being under fire by the school faded. Other parents were seeing what Joseph had to offer, as well. At a back-to-school night function, a mom who had spent time in the classroom excitedly told me, "I just can't wait to see what this kid becomes!" We couldn't, either, and we were looking for any way we could to see things turn out the best way they could.

Some of the anxiety held on to us: If the phone rang during the school day, we jumped and felt the dread that the school was calling with some fresh problem. At home, Jeanne was losing sleep over whether Joseph might be hiding a problem from us. He seemed so much better on the surface, but could he still be talking to himself—something he had done when hearing voices—after the lights went out? When we asked if he still heard them, he'd emphatically say no. Was he just telling us what we wanted to hear?

We bugged his room. Well, we bought a baby monitor and tucked it away behind his bed. All we heard was regular breathing. Over time, we realized that he was sleeping, and that things were actually improving. The voices had indeed receded. He indirectly confirmed it one evening as he sat on the couch with Jeanne. His eyes got wide and he said, "I'm hearing voices."

Jeanne listened. "Crickets," she said. "You're hearing crickets. I hear them, too." Joe relaxed, and she was comforted, too: "It meant that he really wasn't hearing voices as much anymore," she said.

With some of the pressure off, at school and at home, Jeanne and I started wondering whether we could find out what other families with gay kids had gone through. This is a nation of support groups; where was ours?

In May of Joe's fifth-grade year, we attended our first PFLAG meeting. The organization's nearly unpronounceable abbreviation stands for Parents, Families, and Friends of Lesbians and Gays, and we hoped that we would be able to find the information we lacked and the emotional support that such groups can offer.

We tracked down the closest PFLAG group in a town just a couple of miles from our home and showed up for the monthly meeting at a big old church. It was a sweet, small group of parents. During the session, each person talked about their experiences with their children; they told their own stories of a child's coming out to them and invited us to share our own. Since our child had not yet come out, Jeanne mentioned our concerns about the stress that being closeted seemed to be causing Joseph, and mentioned his problems like his previous withdrawal from school social life and class work.

One of the other fathers grew wistful for a moment. "Yeah," he said. "My son did the same thing—he didn't do any schoolwork in class for three years." There was comfort in that: Joe may be different from the other kids at his school, we thought, but maybe he's not so different from other gay kids.

The group was friendly, and we chatted over the inevitable cookies afterward. But we felt that this chapter of PFLAG wasn't for us. Almost all of the other parents were a good twenty years older than we were, and their kids had come out decades before—mostly in adulthood—in a very different, more restrictive time. These parents had been, in large part, bewildered by their children's sexual orientation and had needed to make their own emotional journey to accept this new version of their offspring. They had shown bravery and an admirable willingness to see things in a new way. But they weren't much like us. We already knew that Joseph was gay and that it did not affect our love for him in the slightest. We had a different journey to make, and these folks weren't going to have the advice we needed on helping Joseph make his transition into a more open and comfortable life.

That meeting did introduce us to an idea that would have a big effect on how I saw Joe's struggle, however. The parents referred to the moment of coming out as a statement of something fundamental, using phrases like, "He told me who he was." Not that he told them what his sexual orientation was, or how to classify him in the taxonomy of sexual types. This was identity, something at the core. It was a thought to hold on to.

A couple of months later, we tried another PFLAG group, this time in New York City. This one met at the Lesbian, Gay, Bisexual & Transgender Community Center, housed in a former school building on Thirteenth Street in the West Village. With a rainbow flag hanging above the door and a mural by Keith Haring in an upstairs bathroom, the Center serves as a home for three hundred groups, including a robust youth program.

Jeanne had learned about the Center some months before, in our usual roundabout way. She had been looking online for resources for gay kids. The search wasn't easy, as she recalled. "Type in 'gay' and 'teen' and you get a lot of pictures that make you want to shut off your computer and wait for the FBI to come knocking on your door."

Rich, my friend at work whose gaydar Joseph had so precociously set off, mentioned that he had been donating money for years to the Hetrick-Martin Institute in New York City, which was formed to provide counseling and other services to gay teens in trouble. "I wish there had been a place like that when I was Joe's age," he said. "I could have avoided years of therapy."

When Jeanne called Hetrick-Martin, they suggested calling the Gay Center instead. They explained that much of their focus at Hetrick-Martin is on youth in crisis, kids rejected by their families and even homeless. The Institute runs the Harvey Milk High School, a public high school that provides a safe environment for LGBT kids to learn. It is a place devoted to caring for kids with few other options in life. The Center, with its broader range of activities and services, might be a better fit for a boy like Joseph.

So Jeanne called the Center, and the receptionist suggested that we drop by for PFLAG meetings there. On the appointed day, we left Joseph home with Sam and took the train into the city. The group was welcoming, and the parents were closer to our age. But the group also had a more aggressive, New York feeling. At one of the sessions we attended, a young man handed out flyers for his one-man show about coming out. The group also had a big helping of the Center's activism: a mom urged us to push Joseph to come out and not wait for him to work up to the moment. "You need to do this!" she said. Once he was out, she said, he could take part in activities like the Youth Pride Chorus, and even participate in videos that would promote the Center. Her own son, she noted with pride, had been featured in a PBS documentary about growing up gay.

None of that sounded like our shy Joe, at least not yet. He still seemed to need a more gentle approach. When we left the meeting and went back down to the lobby, Jeanne looked through the brochures and flyers on a rack near the door and discovered the Center's Youth Enrichment Services, which goes by the promising acronym YES. It seemed to be exactly what we had hoped to find there.

"We really just stumbled on it," she recalled. They have a teen discussion group, drop-in counseling, classes on subjects like "Lyfe Skillz," and much more. There was a camp! Or, as the website put it, "a week-long residential camp designed to empower lesbian, gay, bisexual, and transgender young people with the support, knowledge, and skills they need to take charge of their own health and well-being." The camp offered counseling but also swimming and hiking, talent shows and crafts. The idea, the website said, was that "because so many LGBT youth lack a support network that is affirming of their identities, we seek to create a supportive network through the camp program and it's FREE!"

These programs, however, were only available to kids thirteen to twenty-one; we would have to wait more than a year until Joseph would be eligible. And there was that other issue: Joe wasn't out.

Jeanne and I joked to each other that maybe we should just take him to the Center and drop him off at a YES meeting, saying "You're here, you're queer—get used to it!"

We had a sense, though, that we needed to wait until Joseph was ready to tell us his own secret. At least we had been to the Center, and we now knew that when Joseph was ready to be helped, they would be more than ready to help him.

Beyond that, we had no idea what to do next. So we did more research. Jeanne combed online support sites for information and ideas. And I reached out to some experts.

I began consulting with friends that Jeanne and I would eventually come to think of as the League of Gay Uncles. There were people like Rich at work, and Jeanne's cousin Jim, who knew plenty about isolation, having grown up gay in West Texas. And there was Brian Zabcik, a young Texan from a small town who had worked at the *Daily Texan*, the college newspaper. He called me when he moved to New York in 1987 for career advice and networking.

I've never been any good at career advice. My own path into journalism always seemed too fluky to serve as a guide to others. I hadn't taken a single journalism course in college. While I was working at the college paper, I did some freelance writing for a small, college-oriented publication tied to *Newsweek*, and when I got out of law school, I snagged a job there. Within a year, I had been shifted into the main magazine. I never made the rounds of small local newspapers, covering sewage board hearings and night cops. It would have helped me become a more rounded reporter, but I skipped that step and really had no idea how other people made it in the world of journalism.

But I'll have lunch with anybody, and Brian was already well on his way with a job at a legal publication in New York. We quickly became good friends.

During our regular lunches over the years, we talked about Joseph and the growing sense that Jeanne and I had that our son could be gay. Brian had offered advice as we went along and told me of his own realization in childhood, long before he understood what homosexuality was, that he was different.

Now I asked him directly: Should we be pushing Joseph to come out? What would he have wanted from his parents, as a gay kid on the cusp of his teenage years?

That sparked a series of e-mails that were bracingly honest and thoughtful—essays from Brian that recounted his childhood and the gradual realization of his own sexual orientation. He has given me permission to share them.

Brian had a sense that he was gay by the age of ten, he said, though he wasn't sure what it meant. He had his first fleeting sexual encounter at twelve, with another boy his age in the local library.

He built up his story bit by bit. In one of the first e-mails, he recalled that, early on, "my parents were actually supportive of their faggy little boy in many ways. My dad never ever criticized me for not being masculine enough." When he was ten and the family attended a neighborhood party, Brian brought along a needlepoint project he'd been working on. "In retrospect I find it amazing that no one suggested that this might not be appropriate" for a boy of his age, he said.

Then there was his first gun. It was Brian's twelfth birthday, and his father brought him out to the garage for a surprise. "I went out and saw the BB gun in its box. Though I'd never really thought about it before, I just knew instinctively that I didn't want to have anything to do with guns. I didn't even touch the box. I just walked back in the house and didn't say a word." His father left the box in the garage for about a week, "I guess hoping that I'd warm up to it," and eventually got rid of it.

The idea of being gay troubled him, he recalled. It wasn't that he was hearing explicitly negative messages about homosexuality—it simply wasn't discussed at church or on television. "I actually had a luxury that Joe won't," he wrote: "the ability to hide in the ignorance of others."

At the same time, by junior high school, he said he was "pretty unpopular" in school and chalked it up to being different. "I didn't act or look like a boy should." And while people might not be saying anything specifically negative about homosexuality, "I did hear the word 'cocksucker' a lot—about fifty times a day" as an all-purpose insult.

*Even though they probably didn't think about whether
I really liked to suck cock, once I realized that I did,*

their words took on added significance. The fact that I actually was gay was one more way in which I didn't measure up. Looking back at my life, I can now see that I had to get other people to stop thinking of me as faggy before I could say, "Oh, by the way, I really am a fag."

The pressure built up. Brian was suffering from what Ilan Meyer calls minority stress. "I knew that being gay would make me stand out even more than I already was," he remembered. "No kid really wants to be different at school. It's all about fitting in. And not just school, but life." As he realized that he was gay, he was "picturing myself in a room where I was shunted off to the side with the other poor homos."

Instead of liberating him, that first sexual encounter at the library terrified him. "Being told that I was gay—both by this boy and by what we did together—drove me solidly and firmly into the closet for the next six years," he recalled. "I thought and fantasized about guys nonstop, but only in the privacy of my own head. I did my best to act straight, which included dating girls." He would not have sex with guys again until he went off to college. Even then, he said, "for several years after I came out, I felt that I had committed myself to a less-desirable life. . . . It took a surprisingly long time to get this feeling—that I was a lesser person somehow—out of my head."

And so, the advice. "If Joe is indeed gay, then he should come out when he's a teenager, and really needs to start dating while he's in high school," Brian wrote. "This is one of several curses of my generation, that we never did what we were supposed to do when we were teenagers—and so adulthood, for too many of us, turned into a never-ending delayed adolescence. Gay kids need to get the raging-hormones thing out of their system at the same time that straight kids do."

He advised against outing our twelve-year-old, however. "A little inner struggle could be good for Joe," he said. "He can keep his secret to himself for another year or two if he wants. After that point, though, if he still looks tortured and he isn't making any more moves, then I'd give him a nudge."

And so, he wrote, after telling his own story, "now I realize I can finally answer your question: What would I have wanted? What could my parents have done to make it easier to grow up as a gay kid?"

A parent today, he said, should be supportive and give general information about homosexuality, with plenty of nonsexual representations of homosexuality in books and movies the family watched at home. He had suggestions, including a series of young adult novels written with gay kids in mind like the Weetzie Bat books by Francesca Lia Block and Brent Hartinger's Geography Club.

Beyond books and movies, he wrote, a child should grow up with gay role models—not heroes but normal people going about their lives like anyone else. "The goal would have been to show me that while sex may be great, relationships are even better."

For that reason he disagreed with the psychologist who said it was okay for Joe to explore homosexuality online. Hard-core gay porn is too readily available and sends the wrong message, he said—it was a message that led him to anonymous sex for a couple of years after coming out. "I think that screwed-up introduction to being gay is one of the reasons why I'm still single years later, which I don't like," he said.

If I had a wish for gay boys today, it would be that they wouldn't be hit immediately by the gay male community's overemphasis on sex, but that instead they would grow up assuming that they would eventually end up in a relationship and that they would learn over the years how to make that happen.

Brian had one more anecdote for me, about coming out. He started telling family and friends once he got to college. His parents, he said, reacted poorly. Some friends responded well. And there was one "really great, A-plus comment," he recalled. He had gone to visit Betty Sue Flowers, a legendary University of Texas English professor, poet, and an expert on myth who went on to run the school's Lyndon Baines Johnson Library and Museum. Brian was talking with her about a writing project one afternoon and told her that he was gay—"not to come out, since she didn't really know me, but to explain what I wanted to write about."

He wasn't expecting a response, but what she said startled him:

"It's a gift."

Brian, looking back, told me, "I would never have thought of that as a possible reply. Yet I immediately knew exactly what she meant. Because I was different, I would see things differently than everyone else, and that would be valuable to me in ways that I would only discover over time.

"It was the first time that anyone had ever told me that being gay would be an advantage, not a disadvantage," he said, "and I don't think it's too much to say that her words changed how I looked at my life."

Joseph needed moments like that, insights. But they couldn't be delivered until he was ready to come out—and to come out of the increasingly stressed, isolated state that he entered as middle school progressed its roller-coaster path.

The fifth-grade teacher had predicted trouble with the less structured environment of grade six. He had suggested to us that Joseph might not be prepared for the many class changes during the day, or for the step up in academic rigor at the middle school.

Despite Joe's good grades, the teacher told me that he wasn't properly absorbing the material, and wasn't expressing empathy with the characters he read about in class. That didn't seem right to us, especially since Joe could discuss books he enjoyed at such a deep level. Like some of the other teachers, Mr. Fifth seemed to be speaking in code; he seemed to think, despite the plain language of the IEP, that he was dealing with a kid who was somewhere on the spectrum.

Joseph recently provided a new insight into the assessment. Back in fifth grade, he said, he tended to skim books instead of poring over them, speeding through works and gobbling up the plot instead of focusing on every nuance. He could get through three books in a day but would later reread them for more detail. Later he would develop a greater appreciation for savoring prose the first time around.

As for the teacher's point about empathy, Joe said he didn't like many of the books assigned for class. Some people might find *Where the Red Fern Grows*, a story of a boy and his canine companions, touching. But to Joseph it was formulaic, mawkish, and manipulative. In an early entry in his assigned reading journal, he wrote, "I am willing to bet that these dogs both die." He was correct; they did. Looking back as we worked on this book, Joseph critiqued *Where the Red Fern Grows* with an archness that Michiko Kakutani might relish: "I hated the dogs. I was glad when they died, because it meant that the book was over."

Moving to the middle school was surprisingly easy, however, at least initially. Joseph had predicted it: In discussing the move, he observed that most of his problems with teachers had stemmed from his having been exposed to them for several hours each day. "I can stand fifty minutes with anyone!" he said. To a surprising degree, he was right.

He was also happy to be getting away from a classroom aide—like us, Joseph wanted to get the same treatment that other kids got, to the greatest extent possible. The therapist was happier, too; he wanted Joseph to have the least classroom support and the most rules that he could tolerate.

Meanwhile, Joseph continued his weekly sessions with his psychologist outside of the school, and had regular contact with an in-house psychologist at his middle school. We continued to advocate for him, and to try to explain him. During the summer before sixth grade, Jeanne sent the in-school psychologist a long letter about our sense that Joseph was gay, and explained that this was an isolating factor for him. She wrote about the bullying by teachers and other students, and about the trauma of the fourth-grade class, and about our surprise that no one in the schools seemed equipped to deal with a child whose problems might have a lot to do with being homosexual.

"We expected that the school had dealt with gay boys before

and it wasn't really necessary to talk to anyone about it," she wrote. We had learned our lesson and were laying things out from the start this time. We encouraged the school's psychologist to talk with Joe's outside psychologist and to share the "Joseph manual" with Joe's teachers. We expected all of the information to be shared with the guidance counselors and administrators.

"I am sorry that this letter is so long," Jeanne wrote at the end of the eleven-page note, "but we feel that too much information is preferable to too little." The psychologist accepted the letter with thanks, and the manual besides. It all seemed to be working.

It wasn't the end of trouble, of course; while things generally continued to improve with teachers, Joseph was still emotionally immature. He made a few friends, at least superficially, but was building a longer list of enemies; he began getting into fights again with other kids. Many of the conflicts were the product of mutual obnoxiousness, with Joe deepening the hurt with dark insults like "I will dance when you're dead." This school, thank goodness, had a higher tolerance for angry words than the elementary school; an assistant principal reassured us that she knew he didn't mean anyone real harm, though she warned they might have to react in cases where other parents might perceive a threat. Over the next two years, Joe rarely got into a physical fight and never started them. But when pushed, he'd push back.

Joe's tension level seemed to rise when I was on the road—and I was on the road a lot as he was growing up. I'd been covering the space program for the paper after the loss of the shuttle *Columbia* and its crew of seven astronauts in 2003, and made regular trips to Washington and Texas over the next year to cover the investigation of the accident. Once shuttles started flying again, I was attending launches and covering the missions from Houston. For two years after Hurricane Katrina devastated New Orleans, I had been making regular trips to Louisiana as well. I handled some of the parent-therapist conferences by phone and missed others, following up with e-mail. My frequent-flier account looked great, but I wasn't around a lot.

Jeanne worked closely with the school to address Joe's behavior. We knew he wasn't blameless, and that he needed to take responsibility for his actions. We also knew by then that things would go best if we approached the school with a solution instead of an argument or a complaint. Jeanne noted in an e-mail to an administrator that physical violence was rare, and that "his biggest problem is his mouth." She suggested that inappropriate comments be followed up with detention. "As long as Joseph is allowed to give his own side of the story and the detentions are implemented fairly and reasonably rarely based on the circumstances, we think this will work well," Jeanne wrote to the assistant principal.

The middle school tried to help. When Joseph got into conflicts with another kid in his homeroom, school administrators simply switched him into another homeroom. Twice.

"I started to worry that we would run out of homerooms," Jeanne said.

Still, Joseph wasn't the worst problem the school had to deal with. As the town's sole middle school, it threw together the populations of five elementary schools. There weren't urban problems like gangs and violence—I had visited a middle school in Atlanta that required every child to go through squealing metal detectors each morning and submit to a backpack search—but the staff was dealing with the emotional fallout of divorce, cyberbullying, and plenty of mental illness. There were cutters and kids with eating disorders. There were dozens of kids with severe learning disabilities. Joseph may have been a major concern for the elementary school administration, but in the middle school he was in mainstream classes and only caused occasional trouble. By their standards, he was pretty easy.

But for us, Joseph's social isolation was a cause for concern. He was still largely the odd boy. Many of the children his age still looked babyish, but he had hit puberty in fifth grade. His pediatrician warned us that early onset of puberty—and, he noted, Joe was very early—could cause problems. The child whose physical changes came early would feel alone in experiencing the hormonal floods and urges that can make adolescence confusing and miserable for any child. By sixth grade, Joseph had darkening fuzz on his upper lip and was growing taller and leaner by the day. His voice broke, sending that lovely soprano he'd been so proud of into an unmanageable baritone rumble. When he picked up the phone at home, people thought it was me, except that my voice isn't as deep.

It all weighed on him: at school, he slouched and shambled awkwardly along the wall of the crowded hallway while other kids laughed with one another and horsed around. PE classes continued to be a source of stress: he didn't feel comfortable playing the games and was still uncoordinated. I had taught him to ride a bike, but he preferred not to. And when Jeanne saw him on the athletic field one day as the gym class played touch football, he was sitting on the sidelines, having twisted himself into a pretzel and rocking slowly. "My kid looked autistic," she recalled thinking. The stress of having to perform physical tasks just seemed to turn him weird.

The elementary school coach had complained that Joseph was uncooperative. The middle school, thanks to the IEP, tried to figure out why. They ordered up testing for motor-spatial disabilities and translated the results—a kind of clinical explication of the word "klutz"—into a physical training program that fit his needs. The special education physical therapist had several students with the same kind of borderline deficiencies that year, so she put them together in a gym glass that focused on movement, coordination, and strength building. There was also an introduction to games that de-emphasized competition, like kicking a ball to one another without allowing anyone to steal the ball or block. It was perfect for Joseph; even better, he shared the class with Penny, a girl he enjoyed talking with. The coach for the class had a great sense of humor, and his behavior improved.

There was additional relief in a group called "lunch bunch" that was coordinated by a local psychologist working with the school. The group, which was listed in his education plan as a behavioral treatment and accommodation, worked to develop social skills. The group included some kids on the spectrum and some who were not. The therapist seemed to like Joe and had good suggestions about gaining some control over his sharp tongue.

He told Jeanne in a note that he was trying to get a message across to Joseph, that it "is okay to make mistakes, it is human and how we learn; but when mistakes hurt others then there are consequences, and to make the same mistake over and over again is choosing not to learn." He recognized that Joseph could be hard on others but seemed to come down hardest on Joseph himself: "I want him to be easier on himself AND others," he wrote.

Joseph and I began taking walks, heading to the ice-cream shop or getting dinner at a nearby restaurant. I was trying to be with him, and it wasn't like we could throw a baseball around—I couldn't throw, and he couldn't catch. We'd just end up in the hospital. Talking was easy as we walked side by side, discussing anything from his latest books to nothing in particular. The important thing was to walk and talk. "Boys need a male role model," Jeanne said. "He needs to spend some time with you alone."

We continued to work to head off avoidable stress. As the year for Joseph's bar mitzvah approached, Jeanne and I talked about whether the ceremony would mean as much to him as it had to Elizabeth and Sam. Joseph didn't want to do it. He had thought through religion, he said, and did not believe in God. This wasn't a shocking conclusion for us; Jeanne is an atheist. Joseph said he had been reading the story of Job, and didn't want to have anything to do with a deity who would ruin someone's life essentially to win a bet with Satan. God, he thought, was "kind of a dick."

I briefly tried to argue him into sticking with the program. His older sister and brother had been excited by the achievement of reading and interpreting the Torah in front of the congregation and friends—and by having a party afterward.

"I hate parties," Joseph said, and we knew it was true. The challenge of learning the Hebrew and chanting the prayers did not excite him, and we worried that the preparations would put him under pressure that could make school a greater burden for him. He was having some of the same problems in religious school that he was having in middle school, and we were looking to simplify.

We went to see the rabbi for our congregation, Mark Kaiserman, to tell him we had decided not to go forward. I set up the visit with a note saying, "we're inclined to let him drop out of religious school in order to keep the equilibrium in other parts of his life." When we initially told him that Joseph wasn't enthusiastic about his bar mitzvah, Mark smiled and said that he knew how to motivate reluctant kids to do the work. We then laid out more of the story: Joe's problems with stress, his problems in school, and the strain of being a closeted gay teenager. Mark, who is gay, was moved by the discussion and our concern. He agreed to drop Joe from the bar mitzvah program and wrote to us that he would be happy to consider a later ceremony. "But right now, the concern is Joseph's well-being and anything that can be done to help him out."

We had acquired another member of the League of Gay Uncles, one who would continue to provide valuable insights down the road.

CHAPTER EIGHT

I was a Martian child too.

—DAVID GERROLD, *THE MARTIAN CHILD*[40]

A s Jeanne and I thought about writing this book, other books that we have read took on great resonance. One night, she handed me a paperback she had discovered a year or so before: *The Martian Child: A Novel About a Single Father Adopting a Son*, by David Gerrold.[41] The author is better known as a science-fiction novelist and as the screenwriter who brought into being a much-loved episode of *Star Trek*, "The Trouble with Tribbles." This book was an autobiographical roman à clef about adopting a son who had ADHD and many other issues— including the boy's insistence that he was actually from Mars.

The book was made into a sweet movie starring John Cusack. The film, though, missed the wondrous element of the story. I don't think I'm spoiling the ending by letting you know that the boy did not actually come from Mars. But Gerrold's exploration of the problem unfolds marvelously. He discovers that his son is engaging in a variant on what one parent calls "a common childhood fantasy—that the child is really a changeling or an orphan and that you're not the real mother."

Ultimately, Gerrold reaches a moment of clarity: the memory that he'd thought he was a Martian, too, and that "back when I was a kid, when I was the smallest and the smartest, when I was getting picked on every day, when I was teased for just being alive, I knew that someday the Martians would come and get me." Once with his own kind, he had imagined, "we would never hurt again, we would never be lonely again."

Did I mention that Gerrold is gay? No? Well, they cut that part out of the movie, but it's central to the book and his own evocation of the strain of not being like everybody else. And you don't have to be gay to understand that your own child might feel isolated, different. Alone on the planet.

It's our job to love our little Martians, whatever it is that makes them different.

What, then, is the job of a middle schooler? Well, there's homework, of course. But the real job of a kid in sixth, seventh, and eighth grades is getting through the minefield of adolescence in one piece. Their bodies are changing before their eyes. To an alarmingly distracting degree, their classmates' bodies are too.

Many teachers will tell you they'd rather teach any grade but middle school, to deal with any other students but these hormonally crazed creatures. The students, no longer children but not yet adults, don't know where they fit in. It can be a time of crushing insecurity and, as my friend Brian noted, a very hard time to be different.

Joseph was finding out just how different he was. He recently told us that, in sixth grade, he had worked up his courage and told another boy that he had a crush on him. Joseph still had not figured out what made him stand apart from the other kids, but he saw the other students starting to pair up and going through the rituals of going steady, so he decided to do the same. The other boy was not gay, but he was—thank goodness—not upset by the approach, and not cruel, either. He told Joe that he wasn't interested, and they moved on.

So Joseph decided to try girls. After all, he told Jeanne, he was just like them! He liked what they liked. But he found that they were also not interested in his kind of boy, and he gave romance a rest.

Had there been a gay-straight alliance at the school, he might have gotten help in understanding what was going on. If any of the therapists he had seen had tried bringing up questions of sexual orientation, he might have come to see why he was having trouble getting started in the dating game. But Joseph was left on his own to work things out, and came to the conclusion, once again, that there was just something wrong with him.

Maybe because middle school is such a time of emotional turmoil for kids, our town had extensive psychological resources to help guide them through adolescence. Along with the staff psychologist at the school who Joseph checked in with weekly, there was the outside consultant who ran the lunch bunch. In the spring of sixth grade, yet another therapist with the school district began visiting with Joseph. She saw in him a kid with potential, but who was still working to get over the trauma of the fourth-grade teacher. He had said some unsettling things to her. Recalling the way he had acted in fourth grade, he told the new therapist that he believed he was a bad person, a "demon seed." She believed he was a concrete thinker who could be more successful now, especially with the level of support he was getting from the school.

She asked how long Joseph had been seeing the outside psychotherapist. Jeanne replied that it had been two and a half years. The school therapist told Jeanne a surprising fact: that Joseph had told her that he and the outside therapist didn't really talk to each other anymore. In fact, they spent the hour playing poker. It's a good way for a therapist to build a young patient's social skills, but those were some very expensive card games. Neither of them, we think, wanted to admit that after a great couple of years, things had stagnated.

Jeanne picked up on the school therapist's unspoken suggestion that it might be time for a switch. The school therapist brought up the idea of working with a local therapist who happens to be gay. She suggested that this new therapist might have a better sense of how to guide Joseph over the tricky territory of becoming more comfortable with himself, and with coming out. She gave Jeanne a name, with a caveat that she didn't know anything more about him other than the fact that he is gay.

Jeanne and I met with the new therapist before bringing Joseph in, as we had with the earlier ones. A sedate, almost gloomy man, he told us that his approach was "gay-affirming." He seemed interested in treating a boy who was struggling with coming-out issues. When Jeanne mentioned that Joseph liked to leaf through the Coldwater Creek catalog, he abruptly asked, "Do you think he's transgendered?" No, we responded, Joseph seemed pretty happy with his man parts.

We set up sessions for Joseph to start just before he entered seventh grade. Joseph and the new doctor seemed to get along, though Joseph didn't have much to say about him.

After three visits, the doctor called us to meet with him at his office. We had been expecting this: each of the two previous psychologists had called us in after about a month of sessions to discuss general impressions and to lay out how they intended to approach treatment. But what he said, and how he said it, floored us.

He sat us down and handed us a box of Kleenex. Then he handed us a DSM-IV, opened to the page devoted to the description of Asperger's. He delivered the diagnosis with what seemed like pride and asked if we had ever heard of the condition.

Well, yes, we had. And we had heard some people apply it to Joseph and had heard others suggest that he had a different set of issues that were masked by outward behavior that seemed spectrum-ish—most obviously, his sometime reluctance to look people in the eye. These behaviors became more pronounced when he was under stress, and we thought we had a pretty good idea what Joe's biggest source of stress was.

I pointed to the page. "How does this description fit Joseph?" I asked, reading the line that described a hallmark of Asperger's: "encompassing preoccupation with one or more stereotyped and restricted patterns of interest that is abnormal either in intensity or focus." This is the obsessive gathering of knowledge on a narrow topic that gives Asperger's kids the nickname "little professor."

The psychologist hesitated, then explained, "Joseph is so bright that he is obsessed with a wide range of things." Joseph had told him, for example, that he has read every book by Terry Pratchett, some thirty novels.

"So have I," Jeanne said. "Me, too," I said.

"He told me he is *obsessed* with grammar," the doctor said.

"He just finished *Eats, Shoots and Leaves*, by Lynne Truss," Jeanne responded, and pointed out that using a word like "obsessed" and showing clinically significant obsession might be two different things. It wasn't as if he was using a red pencil on the daily newspaper.

The therapist explained that the diagnosis does not depend on having every attribute of the condition but was drawn from a combination of factors. Joseph, he said, had enough of the characteristics that he was confident in his assessment. He noted that the definition included poor motor skills, and Joseph certainly had those. But Jeanne and I had been clumsy children. Sam, who was cursed to inherit it from the two of us, needed occupational therapy to grow into his athleticism. Now Joe's clumsiness meant he had Asperger's?

The doctor's verdict—a verdict, because he explained that there really wasn't much he could do as a psychologist for an Asperger's patient, and that Joe could never really enjoy a normal life—was arrived at with the aura of speed dating, as if he'd just read Malcolm Gladwell's bestseller *Blink* and had decided that it sounded like a terrific idea. Joseph would never be able to go to college, he said, and probably wouldn't even be able to deal with summer camp.

I asked: What about the question of homosexuality?

"I don't think that he *is* gay," the therapist said.

If I recall correctly, by that point our mouths were actually hanging open. The therapist told us that he thought we were overinterpreting things. As an example, he reminded me that I had told him Joseph "never looked at girls in the mall," and suggested that this showed how slender the evidence was that I had used in deciding that my child is homosexual.

Again, we were startled. If that was all we had observed, it certainly would have qualified as jumping the gun. But we had told him about many other things, including the Barbies, the boa, and the telltale browser history.

Luckily, a psychologist's hour is only fifty minutes. We handed back the DSM-IV and the box of Kleenex, thanked him, and drove home, shaking our heads and trying to figure out what had just happened.

I was confident that I had never talked with the therapist about taking Joseph to the mall or discussed whether Joseph was looking at girls there. Besides, he did look at girls. All the time. And then he'd comment on their clothes.

The doctor, we decided, must have confused Joseph with another patient and had gotten his notes mixed up. Maybe he speed-read them. In any case, he was clearly more interested in slapping a label on Joseph than in getting to know him. Or us.

Besides, where was his gaydar?

We left a message on his answering machine telling him that we wouldn't be going back.

Jeanne and I continued to talk about the speedy therapist, and the fact that we had encountered some professionals like him who believed Joseph had Asperger's, while others, including the in-school psychologists and many of his teachers and family friends, seemed just as sure that he did not. To this second group, Joe's problems lay elsewhere, in the subtle learning disabilities that had shown up in testing and in his tendency toward anxiety. Over the years, kibitzers had offered flavor-of-the-month diagnoses that included ADHD, sensory integration dysfunction, oppositional defiant disorder, and bipolar disorder.

Jeanne summed the conflict over the two conflicting views

of an Asperger's diagnosis this way: "'I know that's not it' is neck and neck with 'I'm an expert and I know what I'm seeing.'"

Some people have found a specific diagnosis liberating. John Elder Robison, the author of *Look Me in the Eye*, said that when he discovered in adulthood there was a condition known as Asperger's that explained the differences between him and others, it was a welcome revelation.

For others, a diagnosis might not be such a good idea, as Dr. Alex Weintrob noted in a letter in 2001 to the *American Journal of Psychiatry*. [42] Following up on a case study in which a young man had been diagnosed as having Asperger's, he wrote, "Certainly one has to wonder whether he has been done a favor."

Does it help to know that he has been given a diagnosis of Asperger's? Dr. Weintrob asked. "Or would he be better off believing that he is a somewhat unusual youngster who has apparently made a rather good adaptation to his 'nature.'"

Diagnoses of behavioral disorders can be useful, but they are an imprecise tool. Some doctors—and some who wrangled with us—deny the imprecision with godlike confidence. We didn't think the diagnosis fit and didn't find it helpful.

The psychiatric community itself was in conflict over Asperger's. The definition of the condition has proved so problematic that the APA is removing it from the next edition of the DSM, broadening its focus instead to a general finding of autism spectrum disorder that gathers a range of conditions and pays closer attention to the severity of affliction.

Jeanne sent an e-mail to me a few days after that last visit with the speedy diagnostician that crystallized what we'd been thinking. "If you take out the obsessive component, you are left with a collection of tics," she wrote, not a coherent set of symptoms of a defined disorder as much as a kind of squirreliness.

And so, Jeanne wrote, "It doesn't matter."

The pro-Asperger's faction could be right. We didn't think so, but we couldn't be positive. The important thing to keep in mind, she wrote, was that those therapists were not dealing with Joseph's curriculum or educational issues; they were focused on his social and behavioral skills. "As long as they don't think he's schizophrenic or psychotic or ADHD and they don't want to prescribe drugs, it doesn't matter," she wrote. "As long as Joseph improves, it doesn't matter. It may be that Joseph will prove them wrong, as he has proven other people wrong. But for now, none of that matters. And we're driving the train."

Labels could still cause some problems at the school, however. We remained concerned that a diagnosis of Asperger's at the school would be used to lower expectations of him and to narrow his options. In fact, the middle school psychologists would tell us that they didn't see him as having Asperger's, and that they believed he could perform at the same level as other kids—that he would do well in college and needed the best preparation that the school could give him. But not everyone seemed to agree.

In seventh grade, the "lunch bunch" therapist, without notifying us, shifted Joseph from a group of about a dozen kids with a broad range of social skills into a group with three other kids, some with profound autism spectrum disorders.

The new group began bickering and arguing, and the arguments spilled out into the cafeteria and chorus practice. When Jeanne called the psychologist to ask what was going on, he acknowledged having made the switch and said that he believed Joseph has Asperger's.

It was maddening. Joseph was becoming increasingly agitated and complained to Jeanne that he was being lumped in with kids with severe problems, but the psychologist was holding him to a higher standard of behavior. The psychologist urged him to show empathy to others, but to Joseph, the others "get a free pass" because of their condition. Joe told Jeanne, "I can't help the way I am, either."

In other words, a diagnosis meant to him that he didn't have to try. It sure wasn't the message we wanted him to hear. Instead of learning that he could improve his behavior, Joseph was being pathologized by the label, which was convincing him that he simply lacked the capacity for empathy. It was a diagnosis that was making him worse, not better. Besides, we had seen so much evidence from Joseph of empathy with friends and family that we knew the label simply didn't fit.

I had always quoted a favorite line from *Hamlet* to the kids: "Assume a virtue if you have it not." Hamlet was telling his mother to practice good habits even if she did not feel virtuous herself, because "use almost can change the stamp of nature." These days we put it more simply: "Fake it 'til you make it." But the thought is the same: we can acquire good habits through practice and emulating the good habits of others. It is part of what makes behavioral therapy effective. It was what had been happening in the first group. It could not happen in the second.

We talked to the psychologist who ran the lunch bunch, and he offered to switch Joseph to another group. But by then, Joseph had soured on the whole enterprise and wanted out. The psychologist agreed, and lunch bunch was removed from his ever-thinning IEP.

We also had to figure out what to do now that our experiment with the gay-affirming therapist had failed. We asked Joseph if he wanted to find a new therapist. He thought about it for a minute and said that with the regular sessions with two therapists at school, he felt that he was getting plenty of mental health care. So we took a break from private shrinks for a while.

It worked, until it didn't.

Following Brian's advice, Jeanne and I were discussing gay topics more openly at home. Not . . . *pushing* . . . precisely. But talking. Out loud.

Using our daily *New York Times* as a source, we could easily find stories to discuss at the dining room table, including legal challenges to discriminatory laws, celebrities coming out, political debates over wedge issues like same-sex marriage.

It was rocky at first. One day, as Joseph came down the stairs from his bedroom, we were chuckling over a story.[43] (We really did chuckle. We're parents, not actors. And the story was written by Jim Dwyer, who is eminently chuckle-worthy.) Jeanne had found a story about a man, Mike Shaieb, who was being fraudulently dunned for child-support payments by a woman he did not even know. He didn't even know how the city got his name. But the letter he received from the city said that if he didn't pay his share, he could be arrested, and, as Dwyer wryly wrote, "he might lose his licenses to drive, fish, or hunt, or practice barbering, accounting, or dental hygiene" under the law.

He hired a lawyer and attended the hearing, where the lawyer delivered something of a bombshell argument. "Mr. Shaieb is gay," she said. "He's never had sex with a woman in his life."

In fact, Mr. Shaieb added, "In my entire forty-five years of living, I have never seen a vagina in person."

That was the line that sent us into a giggle fit, and which we read out loud to Joseph.

He got stormy. "What's so funny about that?" He ran back upstairs and slammed the door to his room.

Bit by bit, we made progress. During the presidential election of 2008, Joseph wrote a report that focused on the candidates for president, and he paid particular attention to anti-gay views expressed by Mike Huckabee.

By the middle of seventh grade, in 2009, I could show him a new video that the humor website Funny or Die had put out about Proposition 8.[44] It starred John C. Reilly, Jack Black, and Neil Patrick Harris, who is easy on the eyes and famously gay. The video itself explored the issues and illogic of the gay marriage fight. As the video played, Joe came over to look at the laptop. He wasn't saying anything, but this time he wasn't running away, either.

We had even signed Joe up for summer camp for the first time. The summer before, we had toured a few, and he lit up during the tour of French Woods Festival of the Performing Arts. This was a place that was strong in musical theater, a growing interest of his. The camp has been a training ground for aspiring actors, singers, and musicians since it was founded in 1970. Its alumni include Zooey Deschanel, Jon Favreau, and David Stone, the producer of *Wicked* and *The 25th Annual Putnam County Spelling Bee*.

We didn't know all that when we took the tour. But we did see kids running around the camp who were clearly, happily gay. It seemed to us the kind of place that a kid like Joe could find out that he was not alone.

More and more, it felt like Joseph was getting ready to

speak up. It was becoming agonizing not to give a nudge. But the advice from Brian and other friends had been clear: this is *his* moment. It's great that you are not going to freak out and reject him and make him miserable when he comes out. But there are other ways to screw this up, and one is by stepping on his moment. It will mean everything to him to reveal himself to you: it will take courage and determination. So. Don't. Screw. It. Up.

Most important, they said, don't be clever, please. Don't lift an eyebrow and murmur, "*Quel surprise*" or say, "Joe, you're the last to know." Making yourself look smart and funny, and having a good coming-out story for your friends, isn't nearly as important as letting your son say this on his own terms and at the moment of his choosing.

We had our spring IEP meeting in April to discuss Joe's progress and plan for the coming year. In a note setting up the meeting, the psychologist wrote, "I, too, think that Joe has made many gains while at the middle school and I am so proud of him."

Academically, Joe was continuing to rise; at the end of sixth grade, the school had recognized his language skills and placed him in accelerated English classes for seventh grade. Now, at the end of seventh grade, he had proved himself capable of bearing the workload and making good grades, and the school moved him into accelerated history as well.

If the school year had ended then, things might have turned out very differently. But we still had two months until the end of the semester, and things started to fall apart. As our sense grew that Joseph was about to pull back the curtain, he was coming under greater pressure at school. He was socializing more and hanging out with a group of boys, but they made the kind of knuckleheaded comments that kids tend to toss around about girls and sex and gays. It wasn't harassment, since they didn't know he was gay. But because Joseph knew he was gay, the comments—and the fact that he didn't feel comfortable participating—increased his sense of isolation.

The pressure was increasing, but the support had ebbed. The school psychologist who had advised us on finding a gay therapist had moved on and was not replaced. The other members of the support team seemed to feel that Joseph was doing well enough that he should be making even more progress. Everyone assumed Joseph was doing better. He was becoming a victim of his own success. In those last weeks of school, however, his mood worsened. His slouch became more pronounced, and he told us that he saw himself growing up unhappy, "a creepy old man, alone."

About that time, a teacher complained that Joe's homework was slipping. Jeanne was confused; she had always monitored his homework, blocking out time when he had to do it, and made sure he printed it out and put it in his backpack so that she could be sure he got credit. Both Joseph and Sam had a tendency to do their work and then not get it into the backpack, or to not get from the backpack to the teacher's desk. So Joseph always flashed the homework at us from across the room as he was stuffing it into his backpack.

When Joe got home that night, Jeanne did a backpack check. She pulled out a crumpled sheet of paper. The words on the page began, "*Lorem ipsum dolor sit amet, consectetur adipisicing elit . . .*" Joseph had been filling pages with dummy text, the kind commonly found in newspaper mock-ups and publishing galleys—and, it turns out, on the Web, where he found blocks of copy to paste into his homework pages. He was going to a lot of trouble to trick us into thinking he was doing his work.

Things, in other words, were getting spooky. Increasingly, he complained that he was having trouble getting to sleep and sleeping through the night. And on one of our walks, he said he was troubled by negative thoughts—not the voices of fourth grade, but still dark and difficult. "I am my subconscious's bitch," he told me.

I asked if he wanted to go back into therapy. He shook his head. "I'm dealing with it," he said.

One night in early June, Joseph finally let me in on his big secret.

Sort of.

Joseph and I had gone to a little sushi place in town that he likes. His mood seemed to have lightened, and over dinner, he told me that at school, he was starting to make comments to other boys that were intentionally homoerotic. "I'll say things like, 'Do you think Josh has any idea how attractive he is?'" The idea, he said, was to shake them up a little, especially the ones who make anti-gay comments and jokes.

His statements, he said, did make some of the boys uncomfortable. "They walk away, but some people ask me if I'm gay," he said. "I don't answer, and let them decide for themselves."

So we talked about that for a while, and I said that his air of mystery sounded like a very Joseph way of cleverly getting a message across. Instead of a direct approach, he had left a trail of bread crumbs, I suggested, so that people who cared could follow them and arrive at their own conclusions.

"Like me," I said.

"Yes," Joe said.

"Joe, is it possible that you are telling me something?"

"I might be," he said. And smiled.

We ate.

"I think that it's great that you told me," I said.

"I didn't," he said.

"Yes," I said, "but unlike your friends, I'm not an idiot." I told him that I thought it was cool that he had figured out a way to tell me so that he could decide whether I was going to be supportive or not.

"Stop talking," he said. "Any conversation with the word 'supportive' in it is just going to get maudlin."

The cut-up oranges came, and the check.

"This thing that you haven't really told me?" I said. "Is it all right to tell Mom about it?"

He smiled again. "Yes."

Just like that.

Jeanne and I were feeling pretty good about ourselves. A successful launch! On Joseph's terms! It seemed to blow the dark clouds away.

Jeanne sent me a bubbly note at work, pointing out that "there are tons of things that he can do now that he's thirteen and out—the magical things we were waiting for," including activities at the Gay Center in Manhattan and "the week-long gay summer camp retreat thingy."

We let Joe's counselor at school know, too. A couple of days after our talk at the restaurant, Jeanne sent a note to the school psychologist.

Hi! This is a rather tricky e-mail. I wanted to let you know Joseph has come out at home, so that is good, and he told me I could tell his brother and sister, which I did. Today I asked him if I could tell you and he said yes. There are a few warnings that go with this, of course, because it's Joe. He really doesn't want to talk to you about it and he absolutely doesn't want to hear anything about being supportive or any kind of emotion at all really. He's still a bit emotionally raw about the whole thing.

Jeanne told the school psychologist that, now that Joe was finally out, we were looking for new ways to find a little local community support. "Just asking, but there is no gay/straight alliance, or club, in middle school, right?" she asked. "I know that he feels very isolated at the middle school."

And, of course, I sent a note to Brian. "Just thought you'd like to know that in the most roundabout way possible, Joe came out to me the other night," I wrote. "And so now we can FINALLY talk about things in the open. Which is a relief. Such a relief."

On June 15, the Monday of the last week of school, everything came apart. Joe's teachers were all but done with their lesson plans, and in some classes the kids were largely left on their own.

Joseph's hints had had the intended effect; by then, some kids had asked directly if he was gay. "I'd say yes," he'd say. That day, he was talking with some boys during the last class period and took up a thread of conversation he'd been pursuing for a few weeks: criticizing the way they talked about girls.

"You're always rating them," he said. "Well, I'm going to rate you. You're a seven. You're a five." The other boys grew increasingly uncomfortable. Joe taunted them. "Are the boys afraid of the big gay man?"

A few of the boys went straight to the guidance counselor to say that Joseph had made them uncomfortable. She did not call Joseph into her office or discipline him—school was out by then—but by the time Joe got on the school bus to head home, word seemed to have gotten around the school.

He had come out in a big way. And it hadn't gone well at all.

Jeanne was on crossing guard duty when Joe's bus pulled up to the stop at about 3:30. On most days, he would stop to talk with her for a few minutes as the kids came and went. That day was different. "He had a weird look in his eye," she said. "He acted like he didn't even see me at the corner when I said hi. He seemed to be sleepwalking."

Jeanne couldn't leave her post, but she would be getting off about an hour and a half later, when she'd have just enough time for a quick chat before having to head off to another crossing guard assignment at the town's annual 5K run.

"I didn't have more than thirty minutes" between the gigs, she recalled. "My day was planned down to the minute. I could talk to him when I got home later, around seven."

That's what she was thinking. No time. But when she stepped into the house, she found Joe in the bathroom, with the pills.

CHAPTER NINE

Joe's suicide attempt had made him a statistic—but the statistics on gay teens and suicide are murky at best.

Solid numbers are hard to come by: Coroners do not list sexual orientation with suicides, and research into suicidal thoughts and attempts among various groups of kids can fall victim to the usual biases of self-reporting and small sample sizes. The results of studies, already confusing, are often muddled in the news media, and can be amplified or minimized by activists and researchers with agendas of their own. The disputes can be heated.

And tragedy has a way of throwing gasoline on the flames.

On September 22, 2010, the year after Joe took the pills, a young man named Tyler Clementi walked onto the George Washington Bridge and jumped to his death. Clementi, a freshman at Rutgers, had discovered that his new roommate had posted a note via Twitter that he had used a webcam to observe

Clementi "making out with a dude." The roommate, Dharun Ravi, had tweeted that he would be streaming the next encounter to the Web, typing, "Yes, it's happening again."[45]

Clementi, a promising violinist, discussed the incident in messages on an online gay forum, writing on September 21 that he read comments written by Ravi's friends "with things like 'how did you manage to go back in there?' and 'are you ok?'" as if the scandal was that Ravi had a gay roommate.

The comments further upset Clementi, who wrote, "I mean come on . . . he was SPYING ON ME . . . do they see something wrong with this?" Clementi wrote on the forum that he had filled out a form requesting a room change. On the morning of the twenty-second, he wrote that he had talked to a resident assistant about the incident. "He seemed to take it seriously," Tyler wrote.[46] Several hours later, however, he left a message on his Facebook page: "Jumping off the gw bridge sorry."[47]

Ravi faced fifteen charges that included the invasion of privacy, bias intimidation, and evidence tampering, though he was not directly charged in connection with Clementi's suicide. Ravi, who pleaded not guilty, was convicted of parts of all fifteen charges in March 2012.

The heartbreaking story, with its high-tech gloss and senseless death, became a media sensation—the kind of story that brings a spotlight to an issue. News reports discussed an "epidemic" of gay teen suicides, lumping together stories of other young people who had tragically ended their lives.

But there's no evidence that gay teen suicide is on the rise, and in fact, the extent to which gay teens commit suicide is not really known. Even the question of whether gay kids commit suicide at higher rates than the general population is still being hashed out by researchers, though most suspect that the rate for gay teens is higher.

I'm not going to be able to resolve these statistical disputes in this book. After reviewing dozens of studies and reports, I have come to believe that the weight of further research will eventually show that there is a substantially higher rate of suicide, and a greater incidence of suicidal thoughts, among LGBT teens than in the general population.

Adolescence is a time of high risk of suicide for all kids, not just the gay ones. The teen years are tumultuous, and many kids feel it keenly. This is the underlying theme of all of the teen angst films, but its universality was captured by Shakespeare as well. If you see *Romeo and Juliet* when you are a young person, it is a moving tale of forbidden love. See it again as the father of teenagers and it can have an entirely different feel: a parent sees a story of teenagers unable to see their way through a problem in their lives and committing suicide in desperation.

Shakespeare did not need statistics to find deeper truths, but these days there are statistics aplenty. The Surgeon General reports that the suicide rate jumps dramatically in the teen years. Young people between the ages of ten and fourteen commit suicide at a rate of 1.6 per 100,000, but those in the fifteen-to-nineteen age group commit suicide at about six times that rate, 9.5 out of 100,000.[48]

As the doctors in the hospital explained to us, girls are twice as likely to attempt suicide than boys, but boys are about four times as likely to succeed than girls. The Centers for Disease Control says that in the fifteen-to-twenty-four age group, suicide is the third leading cause of death, accounting for 12.2 percent of all deaths annually. Citing figures from 2009, the CDC said that nearly 14 percent of high school students "reported that they had seriously considered attempting suicide during the twelve months preceding the survey," and nearly 7 percent of them reported actually having attempted suicide during that period. Luckily, the CDC stated, there are as many as two hundred attempts for every successful suicide.[49]

It's easy to see why, when adolescence can be so troublesome. Tender psyches that haven't yet been toughened by experience can be profoundly affected when young love goes badly or when they are hit with any of life's other downturns. The ability to master impulses comes with maturity, which generally emerges later.

Within that bumped-up rate of suicide in the teen years, many studies do suggest that a greater proportion of gay teens kill themselves or consider the act than do their counterparts in the general population. Some of the studies find a difference of twofold, threefold, or even greater. A study published in 2011 by Mark L. Hatzenbuehler at Columbia University that looked at the lives of 32,000 eleventh-grade students in Oregon found that the lesbian, gay, and bisexual kids were more than five times as likely to have attempted suicide in the previous twelve months than their heterosexual peers—21.5 percent versus 4.2 percent.[50]

According to one of the more conservative studies from 2001 in the *American Journal of Public Health* that looked at students from grades seven to twelve, the lesbians, gays, and bisexuals were more than twice as likely to have attempted suicide than the general population of their peers. The percentage of attempts was 17.6 percent for gay and bisexual boys and 14.4 percent for lesbian and bisexual girls.[51]

Some research, however, suggests that there may be no actual elevated suicide risk among gay teens. Brian Mustanski, the founding director of IMPACT, the LGBT health and development program at Northwestern University, found a far lower rate. Six percent of the LGBT youth in the study had attempted suicide in the past year, a rate "that is comparable to other urban, minority youth," as he put it in an article describing his research that appeared in *Psychology Today.*[52] His sample is 264 LGBT kids with an average age of eighteen, and he acknowledges that the sample chosen and their demographics are important. Their incidence of mental disorders was "much higher" than national data on young adults but comparable to the rates of urban youth.

He added, "There is still a lot for us to learn about the mental health of LGBT young people."

Whatever the suicide rate among gay youth might turn out to be, the obvious point is that most of them do *not* commit suicide, and are mentally healthy. In Professor Mustanski's paper, for example, he found that while 10 percent of the kids he studied met the criteria for post-traumatic stress syndrome and 15 percent met criteria for major depression, about 70 percent of those studied "did not meet criteria for any mental disorders." He stressed this positive thought: "One of the most important findings from our work is that most of these youth are not experiencing mental disorders."

This is the point that Ritch Savin-Williams of Cornell has focused on in his impassioned work: most gay kids do very well.

In our interview, Professor Savin-Williams told me that there is a risk of "suicide contagion" in focusing too much on the message of doom and gloom in the news media. The question for those trumpeting the threat of gay teen suicide, he said, is: "Are you actually promoting the very thing you are trying to prevent?"

In *The New Gay Teenager*, he wrote, "If they listened to us experts, I feared they'd be apt to give up, reach the conclusion that their life was inevitably distraught, perhaps even kill themselves."

Suicide contagion is real. Intense and graphic coverage of suicide has been linked to copycat suicides by vulnerable people. It's also known as the Werther effect, a term coined by the sociologist David Phillips. He noted that many men in Europe in the late 1700s committed suicide in the manner of the young protagonist in Goethe's *The Sorrows of Young Werther*, which led to bans on the book. The Annenberg Public Policy Center has even issued guidelines that call for responsible reporting of suicide without the kind of sensationalism that can make things worse.[53]

What the guidelines do not say is that suicide should be ignored, or the news of real risk suppressed. Professor Mustanski, in his essay in *Psychology Today*, wrote that "the prevalence of mental disorders and suicidal behaviors are sufficiently high to warrant special attention to the needs of LGBT youth." By his figures, nearly a third of lesbian, gay, bisexual, or transgender youth will make a suicide attempt at some point in their life—and that, he said, "is too high no matter what the rate is in heterosexual youth."

Of course, one is too many. And if that one child is our son, well, you can imagine how we feel about the squabbling over the precise rate of statistical prevalence.

A large body of research also suggests that the rate of

mental disorder and suicide can be affected by environment, especially bullying. In a national survey of middle school and high school students by the Gay, Lesbian and Straight Education Network (GLSEN), 85 percent said they were verbally harassed because of their sexual orientation, and 40 percent said they had been pushed or shoved. Nineteen percent were "punched, kicked, or injured with a weapon." Two-thirds of them felt unsafe at school, and nearly a third reported skipping at least one day of school in the past month because of safety concerns. The group polled 7,261 students between the ages of thirteen and twenty-one around the nation, about 60 percent of whom identified themselves as gay or lesbian.[54]

College is not necessarily a more welcoming environment, according to a survey released in 2010 by Campus Pride, an activist group that encourages gay students to become student leaders. That survey found nearly a quarter of LGBT students were likely to experience harassment—twice the percentage experienced by their straight counterparts. Nearly two-thirds of the gay kids reported being the target of derogatory remarks.[55]

The bullying has an effect, and gay kids are targets. A 2006 study of 528 "gender atypical" lesbian, gay, and bisexual youth found that 80 percent of them had suffered verbal barbs, and it got physical with 11 percent. Nine percent of them showed symptoms of post-traumatic stress disorder.[56]

Of course, bullying is a common phenomenon for kids of all kinds, whether the thing that makes them different is sexual orientation, race, appearance, or some other factor. A 2007 study funded by the National Institutes of Health found that

89.5 percent of students between third and sixth grade reported having been bullied by their fellow students. What's more, 59 percent of the kids in the study said they had participated in some form of bullying.[57] The report, in the *Journal of Developmental & Behavioral Pediatrics*, was based on a survey of 270 children at three elementary schools. It's a small sample but one that suggests bullying is just about ubiquitous. The hurt lasts: ask any middle-aged man who was bullied as a child what he remembers, and you'll likely get the bully's first and last name.

What the focus on bullying misses, however, is that it's not necessary to have bullies in your life to feel emotional distress. So while the death of Tyler Clementi focused welcome attention on the problem of homophobic bullying, it's important to keep Ilan Meyer and his testimony in the Proposition 8 trial about minority stress in mind. Actual harassment provides only one kind of minority stress; gay kids can carry around an internal bully that makes them feel miserable whether or not someone is picking on them personally.

Minority stress can be made worse when homophobic language is simply floating around and not directed at any one kid. The survey published in 2010 by GLSEN found that more than 72 percent of the gay students said they frequently heard homophobic comments like "faggot" at school, and nearly 90 percent of them heard the word "gay" used in a negative way, as in "that's so gay." Nearly 87 percent of them reported that they were distressed to some degree by the language—as Joseph was.

GLSEN, which has been surveying students for a decade, reported that there had been a steady decline in the frequency of hearing homophobic remarks from 1999 to 2003, but between 2005 and 2009 that progress leveled off. The prevalence of harassment and assault of the gay kids, however, has stayed relatively consistent at about 25 percent.

School isn't the only environment that's important. How a gay kid is treated by family makes an enormous difference. Caitlin Ryan of San Francisco State University and colleagues wrote in the journal *Pediatrics* that psychological problems skyrocket among LGBT young adults who experienced high levels of parental rejection. The rejected kids were six times more likely to suffer from high levels of depression, and were eight times likelier to have attempted suicide, according to the study.[58] Ryan has gone on to create the Family Acceptance Project, which notes the fact that kids are coming out at younger ages, which "significantly increases risk for victimization and abuse in family, school, and community settings."[59] The group's goal, then, is to strengthen families to avoid rejection and to help buffer the child from being too harshly affected by whatever happens in the outside world.

The attitudes of the broader community, which are reflected in its schools, make a difference as well, according to the fascinating study by Mark Hatzenbuehler of Columbia.[60] He compared the Oregon counties in the study and found that the gay kids living in a social environment that was more supportive of gays and lesbians were 25 percent less likely to attempt suicide than the gay kids who lived in less supportive environments.

Hatzenbuehler and his colleagues looked at five elements of life in the thirty-four Oregon counties they studied, including specific policies prohibiting bullying and discrimination, the proportion of schools with a gay-straight alliance or similar club, the prevalence of same-sex couples, and the proportion of Democrats in the county.

Schools that adopted policies against bullying and discrimination, and that worked to protect lesbian, gay, and bisexual kids, saw the risk of attempted suicide by those kids dropped by 20 percent.

You know what happened next: much of the news coverage focused on the juicy political implications of the study. "The bluer the Oregon county, the lower the gay-teen suicide rate," read an item on a *Los Angeles Times* political blog.

Hatzenbuehler sighs when he talks about it. Speaking about the intense media focus on the political implications of the study, he said, "I think that missed the point."

The point, he explained, is that "when schools implement these kinds of programs and these kinds of policies, we see a reduction in suicide attempts." And not with gay kids alone: the schools that focused on bullying and harassment saw a 9 percent reduction in suicide attempts of straight kids across the board.

So, he said, "We need to think about some policy-level changes that can improve and change the social climates in which youth are spending so much of their time."

The politics, then, is beside the point. "Red state, blue state, Democrats versus Republicans—people get entrenched in their different camps and see things as intractable. These results provide a road map for, I think, how we can begin to reduce suicidal attitudes in gay youth." For all the complications people may try to read into such things, "it's simple, from a social science perspective," he said.

Hatzenbuehler's work shows how a community can improve the lives of kids with policies that fight bullying and discrimination. A lawsuit filed in July 2011 suggests what can happen when a school district goes in the opposite direction and actively discourages those policies.[61]

Several activist legal groups filed the lawsuit on behalf of Minnesota families. They argue the Anoka-Hennepin School District, in the suburbs north of the Twin Cities, enacted what they called a "gag policy" on discussion of gay issues and contributed to the suicides of several teenagers in the community. The district's "sexual orientation curriculum policy" stated that:

> *Teaching about sexual orientation is not a part of the District adopted curriculum; rather, such matters are best addressed within individual family homes, churches, or community organizations. Anoka-Hennepin staff, in the course of their professional duties, shall remain neutral on matters regarding sexual orientation including but not limited to student-led discussions.*

The practical effect of the policy, according to the suit, was that the district ignored bullying and blew off attempts to report it. One student said that she was told to "lay low" when she complained to an associate principal about being bullied for being gay; a school official told another one to "ignore" the harassment while another advised a kid to "try to stay out of people's way." All three students are now plaintiffs in the suit.

The harassment, according to the lawsuit, was a factor in at least four suicides by gay kids between November 2009 and July 2010 (and as many as nine suicides overall, according to media reports).[62] [63] The unhealthy environment and lack of support led some of the students named in the suit to consider suicide, or to attempt it, themselves.

The school district denied that the policy absolutely prohibits speech about gay issues. Mary Olson, a spokeswoman for the school district, told Minnesota Public Radio that "teachers are allowed to speak about homosexuality as long as it is age appropriate, fact-based, and related to the curriculum, and that they remain neutral."[64] The district said that students who harass others are disciplined, but that it could not reveal the details of that discipline—even to the families of the harassed students—because of privacy laws.

Anoka-Hennepin School District is within the congressional district of Rep. Michele Bachmann, a Republican with a strong following among Tea Party conservatives. Her husband, Marcus Bachmann, is a psychologist who offers what his website calls "Christian counseling."[65] His practice, according to some reports, pushes faith-based reparative therapy, though Marcus Bachmann has denied it. [66] [67] [68]

In this case, at least, the political linkage makes sense in connection with the community: the school policy was the result of conservative, anti-gay organizations that oppose same-sex marriage and consider gay-straight alliance groups and anti-bullying statutes to be harbingers of a homosexual agenda and promoting what they see as a gay lifestyle. Like so many other things, anti-bullying initiatives were being swept into the culture wars.

A representative of the Minnesota Family Council, responding to the legal attack on the school rule, told the *Minnesota Independent* that the important underlying issue is "homosexual indoctrination."[69] Speaking to the *Minneapolis Star*

Tribune of the issue of how to address gay and lesbian kids in school, he said, "I don't think parents want their kids indoctrinated in homosexuality."[70]

In February 2012, the school district ditched the neutrality policy in favor of a new "respectful learning environment" policy requiring that district staff "affirm the dignity and self-worth of students," regardless of "race, color, creed, religion, national origin, sex/gender, marital status, disability, status with regard to public assistance, sexual orientation, age, family care leave status or veteran status."[71] The next month, the school district reached a settlement with the students who had sued and with the federal government, which had been conducting an investigation based on allegations of civil rights violations through the neutrality policy; the agreement includes five years of federal monitoring for the district.[72] But the groups that favored the neutrality policy in the first place denounced the decision. The Minneapolis *Star-Tribune* quoted a spokeswoman for the Parents Action League, Laurie Thompson, who called the settlement a "travesty" and said that the lawsuit was intended to "abolish conservative moral beliefs about homosexuality." She added, "Making schools safe for 'gay' kids means indoctrinating impressionable, young minds with homosexual propaganda."[73]

This notion that anti-bullying efforts are actually invidious programs to promote homosexuality in schools has slowed or even blocked anti-bullying initiatives around the country. In Michigan, Kevin Epling has fought for six years to pass a state law that would require a tough stance by schools on bullying. It's called Matt's Safe School Law and was named for Kevin's son Matt, who committed suicide at fourteen after a hazing incident.

In 2011, as the bill moved through the state legislature, a conservative lawmaker added a provision that allowed people accused of harassment to claim that "a sincerely held religious belief or moral conviction" underlies their statements.[74] Supporters of the original bill cried that the tweak had transformed Matt's Law into a protect-bullies act.

I called Kevin Epling, who told me that the legislative move was disheartening. "It was done behind closed doors, and nobody knew about it 'til it hit the floor," he said. The argument used to support the added provision was the same as the Family Research Council's: that the creation of special classes of people promoted some kind of nefarious gay agenda.

"They said it's all about sexual orientation," he said. "A Trojan horse."

The hypocrisy galled him. The conservatives had been fighting what they called efforts to create a "specially protected class" of gay kids. "So the first thing they do is put in a specially protected class?"

Matt, he noted, wasn't even gay—the bill, for Kevin, wasn't about sexual orientation at all. "It's all about safety," he said. "I want to be a voice not just for those we've lost but those we don't want to lose."

The long fight, Mr. Epling said, meant there was no end to the family's grieving for their son. "We have lived our loss over and over and over again, every time we've gone to testify," he said. "Every time we've gone down to speak with elected officials. Every time there's a rally."

Outcry over the change led legislators to remove the religious views exception and finally pass the bill in December 2011.

Mr. Epling said that the hard part comes after passage, as the schools begin to implement the new law, deal with the policies, and educate the students, teachers, and parents. It will take time, effort, and energy, he said, along with a commitment from the community.

"Maybe we should get PTOs and PTAs out of the business of selling gift-wrapping paper," he said, "and into dealing with the schools on issues that come up on a daily basis."

Moving forward is going to take leadership on many levels. Debra W. Haffner, a Unitarian minister and sexologist (as she says on her blog, debrahaffner.blogspot.com, "Yes, those words do go together!"), has written that it is time to act in order to save our kids. In a column she writes for the *Washington Post*'s *On Faith* blog, she told religious leaders to "come out with your support for GLBT youth and adults."[75]

In the column, she quoted the German theologian Dietrich Bonhoeffer, who died in a Nazi concentration camp in 1945. "Silence in the face of evil is itself evil; God will not hold us guiltless. Not to speak is to speak. Not to act is to act."

So, she concluded, "It is time for all of us to act."

CHAPTER TEN

Come on, Joseph. One more sip. Come on. One more little bit."

He was choking and sputtering angrily as I lifted the cup to his lips and urged him to drink.

"Come on. Just a little more."

I couldn't help but remember feeding him as a baby. This big thirteen-year-old lying in an emergency room bed was as insensible as an infant, and was just as hard to coax. The cup was brimming with a thick, inky solution of activated charcoal. It must have tasted terrible (the flavor has been compared to sucking on a briquette), but every unpleasant sip was important. The charcoal had to absorb the overdose.

We had been in the hospital for a couple of hours at that point, with doctors and nurses in and out to check on Joseph and to talk with us. They would ask what happened, and Jeanne would tell the story once again.

When Jeanne raced into the house that afternoon, expecting to grab a quick bite and run out to help with the race, she called up to Joseph to tell him what was going on and when she would be back.

"Joseph!"

No answer. There were sounds of bumping and thumping coming from the bathroom, the kind of sounds that accompany flailing around. Finally, he answered, but he wasn't making any sense.

"Books are falling off the desks," he said. "The books are falling off the shelves." His voice was slurred, sluggish.

Jeanne says a shock went through her. "He's on drugs!" Then a thought: *How can he be on drugs? He isn't social enough to score drugs.* How could he even buy drugs? He had no money of his own; none of our kids had gotten allowances; we had always just given them money as they needed it. Jeanne decided he must be sick, and banged on the bathroom door and used the serious Mom Voice.

"Joseph, open this door! NOW!"

He opened the door. He was wide-eyed. And naked. This was a second shock: Joseph is so private and shy that he goes into his room and shuts the door to change his shirt.

Jeanne ordered him to his room to get dressed, and she went into the bathroom to see what he had been up to. It was a mess. The floor was scattered with pill bottles and opened bubble packs. There was Benadryl, and another kind of Benadryl with acetaminophen (the generic drug in Tylenol) and aspirin, along with other over-the-counter meds. We have never had a lot of prescription drugs in the house, but we've always kept Benadryl around. Jeanne is asthmatic and susceptible to colds and flu, so it's helped her through many miserable nights. We also used it to help the kids through colds, or to help them get to sleep when a glass of warm milk didn't do the trick.

Along with the mess of pills, there was a third shock: a knife. It was a paring knife from the kitchen, sitting incongruously in the empty bathtub.

Joseph came out of his room, dressed but dazed. "Sit down!" she barked. "Don't move an inch!" He came into the living room and sat on the easy chair, goggle eyed, while Jeanne went back to the bathroom to take a closer look at the pill bottles and packets. She couldn't be sure, but he hadn't seemed to have opened anything but the Benadryl. She called poison control and asked what to do if a child has taken what appeared to be dozens of Benadryl tablets, along with who knows what else.

The stranger on the other end of the phone took a deep breath and responded calmingly, but there was no mistaking the urgency in his voice.

"You need to call the hospital," he said. "Right now." He asked which hospital we would use, and told her that he would call ahead to let them know she was on her way.

"I don't know," Jeanne said. "I have to call my husband. I have to take a minute and think." She thanked him and hung up.

Then she called me.

I told her I'd meet her at Saint Barnabas Medical Center in nearby Livingston. We knew that emergency room well, thanks to Sam's frequent sports injuries.

We decided not to call an ambulance. Jeanne would get to the hospital just as fast, and we didn't know whether our insurance would cover it.

I told her I loved her. We hung up. I got up to tell my boss that my life had changed.

On the train home, I plugged my wireless card into my laptop and looked up "Benadryl overdose" to see what we were up against.

"Anticholinergic toxidrome," the websites called it. Overdoses of drugs like Benadryl are rarely fatal but can cause delirium, hallucinations, psychosis, dilated pupils, fever, flushing, seizures, coma—a collection of bad effects that medical students have boiled into a mnemonic:

> *Blind as a bat*
> *Red as a beet*
> *Mad as a hatter*
> *Hot as a hare*
> *Dry as a bone.*

As Jeanne got ready to herd Joseph into the car and drive to Livingston, her mind was racing, bouncing. What would happen when the school found out he'd tried to hurt himself? Just a few weeks before, the IEP team had been jubilant about his progress and were talking about putting him into accelerated classes. Would we be back at square one? Could he face expulsion under the "threat to himself and others" clause we'd been threatened with just a few years before? Should she call the ambulance anyway? What would the neighbors say? Would the hospital call the police? Or the school? It was all too much.

She hustled him out the door and headed toward the hospital.

On the way, Joseph drifted into a moment of lucidity. Jeanne asked, "What the hell were you doing in there?"

He said that he'd planned to take an overdose of pills, and

then he was going to lie down in the bathtub and slash his wrists to finish the job. When he heard her come into the house, he said, he tried to hide the bottles and packets by sweeping them onto the floor and hiding them under the sink—that was the thumping and bumping Jeanne heard.

He drifted off again.

Jeanne made it to the hospital quickly, and then found herself in intake limbo. A nurse took down the basic information about the overdose and asked Joseph a series of questions, such as "what day is it?" He stared, his eyes wide. He muttered incoherently.

Jeanne said, "There's no point to this. Look at him—he can't tell you anything!" The nurse called over the intercom to doctors, and then sent Jeanne and Joe back into the waiting area, the place where panic and tedium partner up to produce a grinding misery. Joseph's face was getting redder, his eyes getting spacier.

Finally, a gurney arrived, and Joe got wheeled into a room and changed into a gown. Doctors came and went, asking what happened and examining our mad hatter while he gabbled about chalk and erasers.

That's where they were when I reached the hospital. A nurse handed me the cup of activated charcoal drink and set me to work getting Joseph to drink as much of it as I could get him to choke down. Bit by bit, he got calmer and less red, but he was still largely out of it. Jeanne and I talked quietly and watched our son; we tried to get him to focus his attention on the television, which was running a *Futurama* episode.

As the doctors spoke with us, they seemed to be trying to figure out whether or not they should consider this a serious suicide attempt. One doctor suggested that Joseph might have simply been trying to get high, as some teens do when they raid the medicine cabinet.

Another took me aside and broadly described teen suicide trends: boys who are suicidal tend to seek a violent end, the doctor said, and are likelier to succeed at killing themselves than girls are. Girls attempt suicide more often than boys do, and commonly do so by taking pills, he explained; a substantial proportion of those girls, however, take the pills as a plea for attention rather than as a serious effort.

Joseph faded back into coherence and sluggishly explained to a doctor what he had been trying to do. He said he read the warnings on the Benadryl bottles: do not take more than twelve pills in a twenty-four-hour period. So he counted out more than twice as many as that.

The doctors decided that this had been a serious attempt and said we were lucky, since Benadryl is so difficult to over-dose on. Because this was a serious attempt, he explained, Joseph would be evaluated by the hospital's psychiatric staff and could be headed to a psychiatric hospital.

Meanwhile, things were settling into the late evening rhythms. The medical crisis seemed to be over; by the doctors' estimate, Joe had stopped absorbing the drugs and the charcoal had done some good; within hours, the drugs and their effects would be largely out of his system. Blood tests would determine if other drugs had been swept into the mix, and whether he'd done any damage to his liver or other organs. It would turn out that the acetaminophen in the Benadryl blend would cause elevated readings on his liver function, extending Joe's hospital stay by a few days.

———

The next day, I sent a note out from the hospital to a friend in the neighborhood, Kim, whose son Jason had undergone years of therapy and had periods of intense self-destructiveness. Jason is a sweet boy and a gifted musician who came out several years before. He is Sam's age (and once had an unrequited crush on him) and is close friends with our oldest child, Elizabeth.

I sent Kim a note saying Joseph was in the hospital and that we might need some advice. She wrote back, with recommendations of support groups and therapists—she and her husband had sent their son to a dozen therapists over the years. Their son was getting ready to head off to college; it was a time of happy preparation for them. But it hadn't been so long since things seemed so dark for Jason that they had been talking about the scholarship they planned to endow in his name after his death.

As the next day came around, we realized that we still did not know what caused Joseph to try to take his life. We had no word on what had gone on during school the day before and served as a trigger. Joseph hadn't explained anything—that first full day in the hospital, he barely said a word to us.

Early that afternoon, Jeanne got a note from the school psychologist. She wanted us to know that the guidance counselor had come to see her and told her about the complaints of the boys. She described Joe's blowup, his remarks to the boys in eighth period, the rating system, and "Are the boys afraid of the gay man?"

She wrote, "I know that Joseph does not yet feel comfortable talking to me about this and that you were wondering about how Joe coming out might play out in school. I thought you would want to know what was happening."

So now we knew.

Jeanne responded to her from the hospital room on my laptop. We had decided not to let the school know about the pills and the hospital until we had sorted things out a bit more. So Jeanne wrote that Joseph was "sick with a high fever" and would not be attending the last week of school. A spring flu epidemic had all but emptied the place out, and a note from the administration the week before had asked kids who were sick not to show up.

Jeanne went on to discuss something that had become increasingly clear to us: the school's policy with gay kids had been, essentially, to ignore them and hope that things turned out well. Ours wasn't the kind of community that was tainted by a lot of direct anti-gay bullying, but homophobic remarks went unchallenged among the kids. There was nothing really positive going on, either: no gay-straight alliance at the school, and no way to tell gay kids that they are not alone. We had seen from Jason's experience, and now Joseph's, that the ostrich policy could have disastrous effects.

So Jeanne's note back to the psychologist carried a touch of the anger and anguish we'd been feeling. "Joseph is trying to come out and he is not doing a spectacular job of it, but the school needs to help him with this," she wrote. "We don't know what schools are supposed to do with gay students, but we need you guys to figure something out so that we can all work together."

We were still trying to get our brains around the enormity of what had happened. *Suicide?* We looked back over the past to see if there had been signs. In retrospect, they stood out with startling clarity. *I am my subconscious's bitch.* Over the previous years, there had been bizarre moments that we had, somehow, explained away. One day during the hellishness of fourth grade, Jeanne had seen Joe duck into the bathroom and throw a scarf over the shower curtain rod. When he saw that she was watching, he whipped it back down and went back into his room. Jeanne was concerned, but the therapist was helping Joseph get his feelings under control. He didn't think that Joseph was a danger to himself, so why should we?

Besides, Joe's dark thoughts had receded rapidly after getting away from the fourth-grade teacher, and things had improved for a long while. Then, one day late in June before the end of sixth grade, Joseph had an angry red ring around his neck that looked as if he'd tried to tighten a belt around it. When we'd asked him about the ring, he concocted a story that somehow involved being scratched by the cat. The explanation was absurd, but we didn't know what to think. He didn't seem especially miserable or even all that upset to us.

I had thought it might be experimenting with what's known as "the choking game"—cutting off the blood flow to the brain for a quick feeling of euphoria.[76] It was something I'd experimented with a little bit in middle school myself, though I'd never tied anything around my neck. I thought it might also be an experiment with erotic asphyxiation, a kink that can actually be found in the DSM and whose practitioners have their own derisive nickname: gaspers.[77] Joseph, I figured, could have come across information on that in his online explorations.

I sat Joe down after the incident with the belt and told him that he was engaging in very risky activity. He didn't have much of a response for me but listened in embarrassed silence, waiting for our little talk to be over. Jeanne believed that these had been inept but impulsive suicide attempts. But they were so isolated that she took a course of watchful waiting: nervous but not alarmed.

At this point you might be thinking, *These people are blind.* In retrospect, the only response I can come up with for you is, "Yeah, that about covers it." In the hospital, we were emotionally scourging ourselves over the missed signals and actions not taken. So, no excuses. But, at least, I can offer a partial explanation.

Between our multitudinous activities and obligations—meals and laundry and deadlines, travel for work and making sure the homework gets done—it's as if life itself is trying to give all of us attention deficit disorder. Many of our friends with kids were probably just as blind, distracted by work and day-to-day stress and keeping their family life going. Our other kids needed raising, too. At the time of the belt incident, Sam had been in his senior year of school, with a dizzying schedule of football games and then wrestling meets and all of the practices in between. During an early wrestling match in his senior year, his opponent's head had slammed into Sam's face, breaking his nose.

(They paused the match and taped up Sam's nose; the Saminator then went back in and pinned the other kid. When the match was done, the coach motioned me over and said with a smile, "Mr. Schwartz, he's gonna need a stitch. Why don't you take him to the hospital?" Sam needed plastic surgery that night but continued to wrestle for the rest of the season.)

The moment with the belt came as we were scrambling to finish packing Sam up so that we could drive him to Penn State for summer classes the school provides to many of its incoming freshmen. Joe rode to Happy Valley with us to drop him off, the angry ring still fading from his neck.

Looking back, Jeanne admits, "We were in denial. That's what parents do. You say, 'I don't know what that was,' and you move on," considering each incident "a one-time thing," she said. "You don't connect the dots."

But looking back, these weren't the only dots to connect. In fourth grade, Joseph had avidly played the game Neopets, in which you raise and clothe a virtual creature. The site deleted his first pet because its name violated its terms of service.

He had named it "Suicide."

The hospital moved Joseph out of the emergency department and into an adolescent psychiatric ward. We met with a hospital psychologist, who told us that our boy was showing signs of severe depression. We should not take him directly home from the hospital, he said; we needed to place him in a psychiatric facility for a couple of weeks for a full evaluation, treatment, and, if necessary, the beginning of medication.

He seemed relieved when we agreed to follow his recommendation—so much so that I asked him what parents usually do. "Many of them do agree," he said. But, with a sad shake of his head, he told us he had just released a teenage girl who had attempted suicide into the care of her parents after they disregarded his advice. "I don't know what will happen with her," he said, with pessimism in his voice that suggested he actually had a very good idea about what would happen to her.

Another of the doctors offered a sobering warning that Joseph might be likely to attempt suicide again. He had shown no remorse over what he had done, and a sense of "Oh my God" after an attempt is a good sign. Joseph, by contrast, seemed to have just picked up and moved on, his affect flat.

The people we met in the hospital had seen so much pain and offered great insights into what Joseph was going through. A social worker who was helping us line up the next stage of our son's treatment said, "It's too bad he came out so young." More kids are coming out in their early teens these days, but "I think that when children come out at this age, they don't have the maturity to handle their emotions, and it is more difficult for them," she said. "If he could have waited until his twenties or thirties, it would have gone better."

Coming out later wasn't an option for Joe, but it was an interesting thought: in your early teens, the kids around you are obsessed with sex without really understanding what's going on. They joke about hooking up and about fags. It all makes a gay kid like Joe—who had hit puberty early and had been experiencing the turmoil and longing earlier than those around him—feel even more isolated and freakish. Without the emotional armor that many of us develop later in life, the pain is even more acute.

We were looking for a place to put Joseph, getting information from the hospital and Kim and checking everything against our insurance. After the few days it took Joseph's body to clear the acetaminophen and for his liver to return to normal, we had settled on a mental health-care facility in a nearby town.

As that plan was coming together, I had to make another call that I had dreaded. Standing in the elevator lobby on Joseph's floor, looking out the window at the parking lot and the wooded New Jersey landscape beyond, I called the summer camp.

We had been looking forward to Joe finally taking the step to sleepaway summer camp, and French Woods, with its emphasis on theater, seemed like a perfect fit. But Joseph's session was supposed to begin within two weeks. He would still be in the hospital, and we felt he'd be in no shape to go in any case. And, in our experience, no camp wants to have to deal with a disturbed child. Elizabeth and Sam would come home from their summer camps with stories about the kids who got sent home; Joseph's emotional meltdowns in the summer after fourth grade got him into enough trouble with the staff of a summer day camp that he was threatened with being expelled unless we got a minder for him. We hired a neighbor's teenaged son, and that summer was saved. I had no such hopes for the summer of 2009.

The director of the camp, Isaac Baumfeld, has a deep, rumbling voice and exudes compassion, with a hint of having seen it all. Since he'd worked as a guidance counselor in the New York City schools and had been with the camp for more than twenty years, he probably had, in fact, seen everything.

I told Isaac that Joseph was in the hospital, having suffered a breakdown, and that we expected that he would not be able to go to French Woods that summer.

"Is he on medication now?" Isaac asked. I said that he would be prescribed meds within days. Isaac asked if he was stable. I said yes—he had come out of the stupor of the overdose. We had brought him a two-volume set of Sherlock Holmes stories and he devoured them. He wasn't ready to talk about much yet, aside from Holmes, but he was more himself, more calm, and I told Isaac that.

"Send him," Isaac said.

I was floored. "What?"

"Send him. We'll move him back to the third session. That will give him a few more weeks. Send him," he repeated. "This is a therapeutic environment," he said. "He'll be better off here than sitting in his room."

I couldn't argue with that. I thanked him. More than once. He was giving Joseph a chance, and us as well.

Joseph was ready for release to the psych facility. He said that he didn't want to go, that he was ready to come home. We responded that it wasn't a choice, and an ambulance took him from one institution to another.

The facility was bland and a bit grim. Behind an electronically locked door there were dorm rooms and a common area where kids Joseph's age wandered around. There was a TV and some games. The waiting room had a large-screen television that somehow, no matter when we arrived, always seemed to be showing *CSI*.

We told Joseph that while he was there, he would get a full psychological workup and would be evaluated for medications. All this would make it possible for him to go to summer camp, which he now desperately wanted to do.

We were allowed to call him twice a day, and I initially kept to the schedule. But after a couple of days, Joseph asked why I was calling so much—he was busy with activities, he said, and would just as soon go about his business as talk. So we backed off a bit.

I checked in with the facility's psychiatrist, and after some discussion she agreed with the first hospital's assessment that Joseph's diagnosis was severe depression. That's not a surprising finding after a child has attempted suicide. But it also explained a lot: depression can be associated with many of Joe's behaviors, including sleep problems, a low threshold for stress and conflict, and difficulty in achieving focus, as well as moodiness and even aggression. It was the one diagnosis that no one—none of the psychologists and teachers that dealt with him—had thought of. And it had nearly killed him.

She also suggested that Joseph had a second, underlying condition: PDD-NOS.

The alphabet soup of an abbreviation stands for Pervasive Developmental Disorder—Not Otherwise Specified. It is a diagnosis on the autism spectrum but is applied to people whose symptoms don't neatly fit into the pattern of Asperger's or other conditions, or as a "subthreshold" condition whose severity of symptoms don't rise to the level of being called autism or Asperger's and which don't necessarily show intellectual deficits.[78] But the condition that had to be dealt with directly, she said, was depression.

We still didn't understand why being a little different should require a diagnosis. Of all the diagnoses that Joseph received, however, we were most comfortable with this one. It most closely fit my preferred diagnosis of "squirrelly." It had the benefit over autism or Asperger's of being loosely defined. The diagnosis meant that this was a person who was different but in ways that did not fit any predetermined category. It allowed for Joseph's non-autistic, non-Asperger's behavior: his desire for contact expressed in a love of hugs from family and friends, his ability to do sustained and above-average work in school. It was a definition with the suggestion to most people of being lightly touched by a spectrum disorder and not trapped in a condition, as the speed-dating therapist had suggested, from which no improvement was likely. We could live with this mouthful of a diagnosis. Besides, diagnoses were seeming less and less relevant over time. With so little agreement and no clear sense of whether spectrum disorders could be treated successfully, we could simply focus on the depression, which was treatable and was having obvious effects.

The doctor then surprised me by saying that she would prescribe Joseph a low dose of a drug I had heard a lot about, Abilify.

I had been expecting her to suggest an antidepressant like Prozac. It seemed reasonable to think that you would treat depression with an antidepressant, after all.

Abilify, by contrast, is classified as an antipsychotic drug from the same family of drugs as Risperdal. Because it is generally seen as having fewer side effects than Risperdal, Abilify has come into common usage in adolescents. But at the time some doctors had begun to warn that the drug was becoming overprescribed. They said it was being given to too many people for too many conditions.

I didn't want to argue with the psychiatrist, but I did ask her why she was giving that drug to Joseph. I mentioned the articles I had read that suggested it had become an automatic choice, and perhaps too automatic a choice.

She responded calmly that she understood my concern, but said that if I thought antidepressants were drugs of a narrower effect that address depression precisely, I was mistaken. Antidepressants affect the body and mind in many ways. Drugs like Prozac, known as selective serotonin re-uptake inhibitors or SSRIs, have been linked in adolescents to a heightened risk of suicide through a mechanism known as activation. It seems that in the early days of treatment in some patients, the drugs might provide energy and a sense of clarity but without removing the self-destructive thoughts. The combination can be fatal.

Abilify had not been linked to this activation effect, and could be used effectively to combat the symptoms of depression and impulse control that Joseph was experiencing, she said.

Giving a child who had attempted suicide a drug that had been associated with a risk of suicide, she added gently, would not be a good approach. Abilify should help moderate Joseph's moods and dampen the impulsivity that had put him in the bathroom with the pills. I agreed that it was worth a try.

As the hospital got closer to releasing Joseph from the locked ward into our care, the medical team said we would need to find a psychiatrist who could monitor his medications. We had already tracked down a psychiatrist who seemed like a good bet.

They also said that after his release, he'd need to attend twice-weekly group therapy sessions at their facility for several more weeks. After he had completed those, they said, he would need continuing therapy—both with a psychologist and in a moderated social group. By the time Joseph was ready to be released, we had a plan.

As we prepared to send Joseph off to French Woods, we sat down with Rabbi Kaiserman again. He had been supportive when I'd let him know what happened with Joseph, and he welcomed us into his office.

He said that coming out can be extremely messy, emotionally—that many kids come out explosively, and with bad results. It can take a while to recover, he said. Jeanne talked about how strangely the school had reacted to Joe's being gay, and she noted that Joseph is "classified," that is, under an IEP. "Well, a lot of gay kids are," Mark noted.

Jeanne took it a step further. "I feel like the school would rather he had autism than be gay," she said. "They seem more comfortable with the concept of autism, which they understand how to deal with."

"Yes," he said softly. "Of course they would. They don't like to think about kids having sex. And they *really* don't like to think about two *boys* having sex"; the idea of penetration just makes them uncomfortable. Even though people have a sexual orientation long before they have sex, he said, society tends to conflate the two.

Mark's comments helped explain why no one in the schools ever seemed to want to take seriously our questions about whether Joe's sexual orientation was affecting his ability to relate to other kids or was contributing to his feelings of isolation. We had told them it seemed to be a key to Joe; they had treated it as irrelevant.

Over time, Mark explained, Joseph would have to figure out how much of his identity would be wrapped up in being gay—"He will learn that being gay is *one* of the things he is, and not the only thing he is." The decision about how much of his identity will be focused on being gay, ultimately, would be up to him.

He asked what we were doing with Joseph for the rest of the summer, and we told him we were sending him to a theater camp. "Which one?" he asked with interest. When I told him it was to be French Woods, he exclaimed, "*I* went to French Woods!" And somehow, it helped us know that Joseph might be okay there.

A couple of days after Joseph entered the psych ward, Jeanne dropped by the school to clean out his locker and pick up his report card. As she waited in the office, the emotions of the past days and the sleepless nights overwhelmed her, and she began to cry. Worried staff members ushered her into the assistant principal's office. The guidance counselor soon joined them. They asked Jeanne what was going on.

The story spilled out, starting with the day that Joseph came out. Jeanne told them that Joseph had suffered some kind of breakdown and that he was in a mental ward. She didn't mention the pills, but she talked about everything else, including the fact that we felt the school hadn't responded well to our concerns about increasing trouble in classes. He had been falling apart, she said, and the school had basically told us that he needed to toughen up. The angry outburst and the rating taunts, Jeanne said, were exactly the kind of situation we had been trying to avoid when she had told them that Joe is gay.

The assistant principal interrupted. "Wait—I'm confused. Is Joseph gay?"

Jeanne was dumbfounded, and furious. "I told you that he was!" she said.

"You never told *me*," the assistant principal said.

"But I told the psychologist! Didn't she tell you?"

How could she have not known, when we'd shared so much with the school's psychologist? It turned out that the psychologist, thinking we might be sensitive about Joe's privacy and worried about gossip, had kept the news to herself. Whatever the school might have done, the news that might have triggered action from the top had stayed behind the door of the psychologist's office.

The assistant principal said that we should have gone directly to her with our concerns and told her ourselves that Joe is gay. The violations of the IEP should have come to her, as well as the psychologist's impatient response that Joseph needed to learn to get along with people he didn't like.

Of course, no one had told us any of that, and lines of authority at the school had never been fully explained. Thinking we had a single point of contact, we focused our discussions with the person who spent the most time with Joseph, and we assumed that she was passing the information along to everyone who needed to know.

With more digging and more talking, the assistant principal was suggesting, things might have been better. On the other hand, she might have simply been looking for a way to blame us for our problems.

Jeanne said, "I am DONE with all this secrecy! We'll just tell *everybody*. I'll send Joseph to school in a T-shirt that says 'GAY' on it."

"No you won't," the assistant principal said with a businesslike, almost stern tone. "That isn't allowed." The school had a policy prohibiting disruptive statements on T-shirts.

That meeting broke up, and Jeanne was ushered in to talk with the guidance counselor. She seemed surprised that we thought that being gay was the source of so much of Joe's distress: "Being gay is no big deal these days!" she said. Everybody watches *Will & Grace* and Ellen DeGeneres, right?

She took Jeanne to the psychologist's office to continue the conversation. All of the teachers, the guidance counselor noted proudly, had received training from the Gay, Lesbian and Straight Education Network on supporting gay kids.

But, Jeanne asked, what about the students? Shouldn't there be a gay-straight alliance or some other group to help the kids in the school recognize that there are gay kids in their midst? The guidance counselor said softly, "The parents . . ." and trailed off. There was a gay-straight alliance group at the high school, but middle school administrators seemed to be worried about what parents would say if they appeared to be promoting a gay club.

So there it stood. It was okay for Joseph to be gay, but he shouldn't be too open about it. No in-your-face provocation.

When Jeanne told me about the conversation that night, I sent a note to Brian Zabcik, once again seeking the advice of the gay uncle. I mentioned to him that the school had said that Joseph would be fine if he was quietly out but not disruptive.

"Ugh, you're kidding me," Brian wrote back. He had become politicized during his early days in New York and had protested with Act Up, a group that staged angry protests to spur greater government action on AIDS.

"That's exactly the kind of mentality that leads kids to either shriek out of the closet or else close the door tighter," he said. Either way, a request that Joseph not be blatantly out at school was inappropriate, he insisted. "That is their problem, and it's their job to deal with it, not yours."

All the people we dealt with at the school had good intentions. None of them disliked Joseph. But they hadn't worked together. They did not have a way to help kids like Joseph and Jason—or parents like us. Kim, Jason's mom, told us the schools had loved her son when he was a successful musician and straight-A student. Once he was derailed, she said, there was little support. There were no programs to deal with the kinds of problems he had, and the help he did get came from individuals who "worked around the system" to obtain services, not the school. "It was the character of the individual people, not the structure of the system," she said.

With so few boys coming out at such a young age, the middle school didn't seem to feel that it needed to come up with a policy to help these kids. The school reached out to parents about so many issues; the office had brochures for parents that helped them deal with everything from helping a child with eating disorders to bullying, but they didn't provide resources that could ease people like us through the process of raising a gay child, with information on the nearest PFLAG meeting and the Gay Center, just across the river.

That only meant there was nothing unusual about this school. Middle schools lag far behind high schools in this country when it comes to reaching out to gay students and their families. GLSEN's 2009 School Climate Survey, the most recent one available, found that while nearly half of American high schools have a gay-straight alliance, fewer than one in ten middle schools do. The survey found that about half of high schools have an environment that is considered to be "supportive or very supportive," for LGBT kids, but just a third of middle schools do.

So as much as we felt the school could have done more, we also knew that our town can rightly boast of having one of the best school districts in the country. The district puts more resources into helping special needs and different kids and is more responsive to individual problems than most schools across the country. In districts just a few miles from our home, there wasn't enough money in the budget for even minimal services. A child of good friends didn't get classified by his school in Maryland until years after the diagnosis of the ADHD that contributed to his terrible grades; his first IEP was drafted during senior year, when he was on his way out the door. In our district, by comparison, parents are heard, though they might have to make a ruckus to get the schools' attention. Once we really started to push, and gained an understanding of the system, things began to turn around. We know that in many schools Joseph would have been lost in the shuffle, and even if someone had picked up on his problems, the accommodations and services wouldn't have been there. In the Maryland school where Joe's brother, Sam, had to slam a kid against the school wall to break a cycle of bullying Joseph would have done much worse.

Joseph got home from the hospital and was still adapting to the medication, which made him nearly frantic with a kind of bounciness that had him pacing from one room to another and back again. He was also ravenous, eating five meals a day and snacking, too.

Bit by bit, however, the side effects receded, and Joseph became calmer—not tranquilized or doped up, but less agitated. He was still Joe but without the intrusive thoughts that had been tormenting him.

Finally, the day to take Joseph to camp arrived. We drove the two and a half hours to Hancock, New York, where French Woods nestled in the upstate hills. It seemed even more beautiful than we had remembered from our tour the summer before. Like other camps that Elizabeth and Sam had gone to, French Woods had cabins and a lake and horses. But it also had a fully equipped gym with dozens of treadmills, ellipticals, and weight machines. It had a soaring steel structure for circus training with ropes, pulleys, nets, and mats. It had five theaters—including a proscenium stage, two black boxes, and a theater in the round. Each summer, the campers and staff pull together more than seventy full-scale productions, some accompanied by orchestras made up of campers who had their own practice studios and training program. Kids also worked in the costume shop and created the elaborate sets.

For Joseph, it seemed like a perfect place. The fact that it was an environment where gay kids felt completely comfortable being out made it even more attractive.

After we found his cabin and packed his clothes into the cubbies, I walked over to the infirmary to make sure they had gotten the shipment of Joe's pills. French Woods accepted medications only through a mail-order pharmacy that sent the goods to the camp in well-labeled, sealed individual doses. When I got there, it was easy to see why they put parents to the trouble and expense: the med shack, as they called it, was a small room off the main infirmary whose walls were lined with shelves, each shelf packed with labeled boxes. The system ensured that there was consistent packaging and labeling and that the right kids would get the right drugs in the right dosage.

I checked in with the nurse and nervously asked whether it was unusual for a kid at the camp to be taking psychiatric meds.

"Are you kidding?" she said with a laugh. "This is a *theater* camp!"

Jeanne and I drove the 120 miles home with a blend of emotions that had become so familiar to us: hope and worry. But this time, hope was winning.

CHAPTER ELEVEN

For the next three weeks, we felt the familiar, small twinge of panic whenever the phone rang, thinking that it was the camp calling with a Joseph problem, or even a Joseph crisis.

Sending him away to camp for the first time had been a gamble, and the fact that he was just weeks past a suicide attempt made it an even bigger one, despite Isaac's confident, wonderful "Send him." Joseph had proven fragile. His older brother and sister were flexible; he was breakable. We wondered what the psychological damage to him would be if he flunked out of summer camp.

As Jeanne put it, "if he couldn't go to camp, how could he go to college? And if he couldn't go to college, what would happen to him?" Was Dr. Speed-Date right after all? We really didn't feel that we could risk a failure, but we knew even more powerfully that we couldn't risk the consequences of not sending him to camp at all.

We heard nothing. I called the camp, trying not to be a helicopter parent but wanting to make sure things were okay. Yes, the camp assured me. Things are okay. They were watching him, and he'd had some angry outbursts and emotional moments. But he was fine.

As the term came to an end in August, we drove back up to French Woods, wondering what we would find. We walked across the hilly camp toward Joseph's cabin. He saw us through the open window and ran out to give us both huge, bone-bending hugs.

He showed us around the camp, introduced us to his friends, and later that evening we saw him perform in one of the shows for that term, *No, No, Nanette.*

"Do you want to go back next year?" we asked.

"Yes!" he said.

He was relaxed. He was happy. He was Joseph. But he was also a little more: he was Joseph, on his way.

As we strapped into the car, it became clear that he was also very smelly. He had worn his shoes without socks during his three weeks at camp, and they—and his feet—had become toxic. We chucked the shoes in the trunk, cracked the window open, and got our boy home.

We wanted to build on Joe's delicate success. The warning in the hospital had weighed heavily on us: the doctors seemed to think he would be back, and soon. Several friends had suggested it was the beginning of a long and potentially hellish road.

We wanted to do anything we could to prove them all wrong.

If we had asked Joe too little about his emotions and feelings in the past, we were now overdoing it. "So! How are you feeling, with the Abilify?" I'd ask. "Any intrusive thoughts? Are the negative urges showing up again?"

Over the weeks, the answer went from "a lot less" to, simply, "no," with a kind of relief at first, but with a bit of testiness as the exchange became repetitive.

I could stand irritating my son. It's kind of my role in life. And we weren't taking chances anymore.

As summer ended and the beginning of eighth grade neared, the first thing Jeanne and I had to work out was what we could do with the gap of about an hour and a half after Joe's school let out but before Jeanne got home. Our friend Kim had suggested from her own experience with Jason that we shouldn't leave Joseph home alone. We agreed: we didn't want him to come home from a tough day at school and brood alone in the house.

We told Joseph that when he got out of school, he should head over to the town library, just a short walk away, and read or do homework until Jeanne could pick him up. He could cross a pedestrian bridge and take a path that led past soccer fields to the library. Once school started and Jeanne began picking him up there, she was startled. "Everybody is dumping their kids at the library!" she said. The place got very crowded after the school bell. Joseph generally found a quiet corner.

There were some initial rough patches: when other kids got rowdy, Joseph would confront them and arguments would start. The librarians told Joseph he'd be kicked out if he kept it up, and I reminded him that he didn't need to be the "cop of the world." This time, he got the message. He liked the library, and wanted to stay.

Before long, he and the kids he sat with became buddies.

They began hanging out together, grabbing a bite before hitting the library. The school was noticing that Joseph had become more social; the school psychologist would tell Jeanne proudly that teachers who used the library as their office for tutoring had commented to her they were seeing Joseph there with his friends.

The other kids were helping Joseph become more sociable, but they wouldn't have been able to reach him if he hadn't been more reachable in the first place. Could it be that coming out at last had relieved much of the pressure he'd been living under for so long? It seemed to us that his walls were coming down.

Joseph was now openly, quietly, gay. And nobody seemed to care. In fact, Joseph himself may well have had something to do with that. When the eighth-grade school year started, the hallways were plastered with anti-bullying posters. The school was stepping up its efforts to promote tolerance.

With the beginning of school, we started another new routine as well. We came into Manhattan on Saturday afternoons to take Joseph to the Gay Center so that he could attend the teen discussion sessions held by Youth Enrichment Services.

We were following up on the recommendation from the psychiatric facility that Joseph participate in a social group, and here was one in which the kids would have something big in common: being gay. Joe was willing to give it a try. So Jeanne called ahead and was told that a new kid coming into the program needed to be evaluated. A psychotherapist, Scott, would be on duty that Saturday and would be able to visit with Joseph, as one of the three counseling sessions that are available to each newcomer.

On our first visit, we walked through the lobby of the former high school and took the narrow hallway to a courtyard, where some of the older members of the Center community were hanging out and enjoying the sun. The YES program was in a separate building across the courtyard, behind a steel door.

As we entered, we saw a reception desk in front of us and kids sitting around on couches to our right. The receptionist stopped us and said this was a teens-only space, not a place for parents. She wasn't confrontational, or even unfriendly. But she was firm.

It was easy to understand why: many parents are upset to find out that their kids are gay. YES has become a refuge for more than a thousand young people and the rules helped them to feel protected.

We asked for Scott, and he soon came out to meet us. He was a young man with a shaved head and a reddish beard; he quickly ushered us out of the teen zone. We told him that Joseph had had a rough summer after coming out but that he seemed to be a lot steadier now. We talked a little about the medication.

He quietly asked Joseph a few questions: do you do drugs? "No," Joseph answered. Have you tried to commit suicide? Joe shrugged and said yes. Scott then asked us to wait in the lobby while they completed their visit.

When they came back, Scott was all smiles and invited Joseph to stay for his first teen discussion group. But the interview had made him jittery. "Could we go?" he asked.

Jeanne and I were worried that he might be trying to back out of the youth group altogether, but Joseph assured us that he did want to start attending the discussion. "Just not today," he said.

The next week, Joseph was ready to try again. We walked him back to the YES center again and he had his first session with the discussion group. It seemed like a good crowd, easygoing and multiethnic—albeit with more piercings and leather than Joseph was used to seeing at his suburban middle school.

In the group, Joe sits with a half dozen to twenty kids; a social worker or peer facilitator leads the discussion. Each session has a topic: Beauty. Relationships. Love. Drugs. Self-image.

The conversation moves around the room, each teenager contributing. If one says something that causes offense, the offended person says "ouch" and explains the offense. The person who has said the offensive remark responds "oops"—not an apology, but an acknowledgment of having caused offense. And the building blocks of social interaction are stacked one atop the other as the kids exchange information.

In the discussions, Joseph quickly earned his share of "ouches." And a couple of times, the discussion would get tense and he would storm out, or the emotional content would be too heavy and he would slip out quietly and wait for us in the lobby. Before long, though, he was cracking jokes and occasionally defending his ouches, explaining himself to the group. Eventually, one of the regulars pointed to Joseph and said, laughing, "I live for this bitch!"

I checked in with Brian to give him a gay uncle update on Joseph's progress, and mentioned that we were visiting the Center. He recalled having attended a gay male support group at UT when he was a student, and said it was "helpful, mostly because I met someone there I could date." That was huge, he stressed: he had longed for the kinds of relationships that his straight friends had so easily fallen into in high school.

He also wanted to make sure we understood that the Center did not represent all gay life and relationships. Gay white males, he explained, tend to socialize in private places like clubs and bars, while blacks and Hispanics, "especially the femmy guys," are drawn to public services like the Center and the Hetrick-Martin Institute.

> *The reason that I mention that point is that when I was coming out, one of the issues that I had was that I didn't want to be like the queeny gays I was seeing. It was very important for me at the time. It was already hard enough for me to deal with being gay; thinking that gay = effeminate was another problem. This isn't an issue for me anymore, and it may not be for Joe at all. But I thought that I'd mention it in case it is., i.e., the degree to which he might be meeting people at HM or the Center who are more different than him than he expects. . . . The youth programs at the Center might have the right mix for Joe. I'm just saying that you should pay attention to whether the crowd at any given place seems like one he's comfortable in.*

Joe was comfortable with the group, though, and we came to love the Center as well. Its detailed calendar shows a rich range of activities among the more than three hundred groups that meet there. There are regular "pride toastmasters" meetings to build public-speaking skills, and groups devoted to spirituality and book discussions. There are recovery groups for those whose families wounded them, and to help overcome addictions.

Gay senior citizens have SAGE, Services and Advocacy for

GLBT Elders. Younger members with a geeky bent can attend meetings of the "Gay-mers group," kids who like board games and nerdy fun. The Center hosts a college fair where schools can tout their rainbow-hued activities and programs. And YES provides its kids with crisis intervention counseling, job readiness programs, HIV prevention workshops, and leadership training, along with holiday fun like the annual Thanksgiving celebration, "Thanks for Being Queer."

For the grown-ups, a fair amount of the Center's programming is geared toward getting people together. Some are there to find a soul mate, maybe to build a lifelong relationship. Others are looking for what Lyle Lovett, in his song "Here I Am," calls opting for "the more temporal gratification of sheer physical attraction."

There's a proud vibe of sexuality to the place—the free packets of condoms and lube at the reception desk make that clear, if not the upstairs bathroom that is covered with the startlingly X-rated mural by Keith Haring. You can attend group meetings for those interested in master/slave sexual relationships, and there are frolics like the occasional dance party known as the "Fur Ball," which bills itself as "a celebration of everything furry and fuzzy."

The Center showed Joseph that he was not alone, but it was also showing him that being gay isn't one thing but a spectrum of lifestyles and behavior. In the discussion group, some of the kids were flamboyant, and some were reserved. Some were transgender teens in the midst of their transition, requiring Joseph to pick up the tricky system of pronouns used in realms of indeterminate gender. Some of the kids came in under assumed names, like Maxie or Bubbles.

Joe's coming out might have been a sensation in his suburban seventh grade, he said, but, "Here? I'm *boring.*"

With so much newfound support and activity, eighth grade turned out to be blessedly uneventful. Maybe a little too uneventful for his taste: he was waiting for other gay boys to show themselves. Statistically, he knew there had to be some, but he remained the only out boy at the middle school—and observed to Jeanne, "I'm the last person anyone would call a trendsetter." Still, he kept his grades up and grew closer to his group of library friends, and before long it was time for graduation.

The ceremony was held in an ice-skating rink in West Orange, New Jersey, a vast and chilly space where several hundred chairs were arrayed in neat rows on a platform over the ice.

The kids lined up to receive their diplomas, shuffling along a few rows at a time. I couldn't help but notice that Joseph was taller than most of the kids now and seemed even taller because he had lost the slouch.

A middle-school graduation is the kind of thing I'd usually joke about, a kind of empty, feel-good moment, inevitably overplayed in light of its actual significance.

But it sure meant plenty to me now. One year before, Joseph had been in the hospital. If we'd kept more powerful drugs around the house, we could have lost him. I felt a fullness in my chest, and it was all I could do not to start crying. Pulling out my camera phone, I took a blurry picture of Joseph shaking hands with the principal and sent it from my phone to Elizabeth and to Sam with a text message letting them know that their little brother had just graduated.

Elizabeth texted back first from Austin, where she had moved after graduating from the University of Michigan. "He's so tall!" she wrote. "I'm proud of him."

After the graduation ceremony, I found Joe in the crowd and we headed back to the car. I turned the key in the ignition and tapped the iPod I had connected to the stereo; the frantic rhythms of the Barenaked Ladies blared out of the stereo speakers as they belted out the song "Grade 9."

Joseph beamed. "You planned this!"

"Of course," I said.

Over that summer, Joseph returned to French Woods, and also signed up to attend the YES program's one-week Community Camp, which is held at a Boy Scout camp in western New Jersey. It promised to be as much therapy as fun, the culmination of the year's work at the Center.

The program requires the kids to be ready for the experience by attending at least four sessions in the weeks before camp, where the campers-to-be work with mentors and peer advisers to discuss what they hope to get out of the experience. Joe's mentor told us that he saw Joseph as a kid with great potential who was too "locked up" and afraid to express himself. "I want to pull him a little outside of his comfort zone," he said.

There was an orientation for parents, too, a question-and-answer session to let us know what would be happening during the kids' week away. The counselors explained that the kids would be grouped by age in mixed-gender cabins. Some parents, they admitted, were a bit uncomfortable with that arrangement, but the camp had found that age was the most important thing that many of these kids had in common. During the session, Jeanne and I sat with another couple who said that they were uncomfortable with what was going on; their daughter was only thirteen, they said, and a lot of the YES discussion focused on sex. The concern seemed almost jarring to us: if your kid is here because of her sexual orientation, somebody might end up talking about sex, right? But it was a glimpse, for us, into what other parents were going through. It also suggested the range of parental concerns that the program had to deal with, and to respect—and perhaps supplied another reason that parents were not welcome in the sanctum of YES.

Jeanne sent a brief version of the Joseph manual to the program coordinator, laying out what to expect. "Conflict and confrontation are poisonous for him," she wrote. "If he becomes upset, let him remove himself and calm down."

The response was comforting. "I monitor our youth in my camp role as Emotional Fitness Coach," she said. "I handle crisis intervention and hold drop-in counseling hours daily. Although the camp experience is very rewarding, it can also be emotional for youth."

The next week was intense. It was in many ways a summer camp—games like tag to start the day, and workshops in arts and crafts. But there were also workshops like the weekly sessions at the Center, along with educational sessions about HIV and substance abuse. Lots of summer camps have dress-up themes at dinner, but this camp had drag night. Evening activities might include campfire songs and making s'mores, but there was also an intense "night of confession" when people told their stories. Some had been kicked out by their families or abused; others had been bullied, even beaten, at school. A few of them had ended up living on the streets for a while; Joe heard about drug addiction and suicide attempts.

He told them what he had been through, and how we, his parents, felt it was important that he be part of a broader gay community. That we had helped him find the Center and YES. And his friends told him, "I wish I had your parents."

Sometimes these discussions were so raw that Joseph had difficulty dealing with the emotions and had to step out of the room; the counselors let him take the tumult at his own pace.

He was up early for the dawn hike and had held on to a surprise for the talent show: an enormous black boa that Jeanne had bought him just before he left for camp. Joseph, the quiet kid, got up in front of the group and belted out an ultra-campy song, "Was I Wazir," from *Kismet*.

He killed.

"Oh my God, Joseph! I didn't know you could *sing*!" one kid said.

A couple of the kids shyly let Joseph know, through intermediaries and notes, that they had crushes on him. He let them know that he wasn't ready for that quite yet.

A few days later, the buses pulled up in front of the Center again, and dozens of tired, happy teenagers piled out, lugging their bags out of the back.

Joe hopped out and, after hanging out and talking a bit and hugging everyone good-bye, got into the car for the drive home.

He had come back calmer, more confident, less tightly wound. It wasn't long before Jeanne signed the family up as members of the Center, hoping to repay the organization that had done so much for us. "They've given us our son back," she said.

Fall was approaching, and with it the beginning of high school. It was another big change, but we felt ready for it, and we felt

Joseph was ready, too. The high school has an active gay-straight alliance. We knew from the experiences of Elizabeth and Sam that a number of kids come out in high school and that most of them didn't seem to have much trouble.

Once again, we had written a manual for the school's psychotherapist: this one was thinner than the ones that had come before, but fortified by the lessons learned in previous years. It started with a bang:

> *First, and most importantly, we wanted you to know that Joseph is gay. He is completely out at school and we would like for everyone at the school, his teachers and the school administration, to be made aware of this fact. While we want to emphasize that Joseph has suffered no discrimination at the middle school whatsoever for his sexual orientation, we would all feel more comfortable knowing that everyone is looking out for him.*

No more secrets! No more miscommunication; we wanted it out there for everyone. And we discussed the learning disability and psychological issues as well.

> *Joseph also has some learning impairments. We have found with him that no diagnosis really describes fully what his impairments are. We are more comfortable with simply describing the impairments and making sure the IEP cover them than trying to bend a diagnosis to fit. However, if a diagnosis is really necessary to accomplish all the accommodations that Joseph needs,*

he was recently given a diagnosis of PDD-NOS. We are all comfortable with having this diagnosis noted in his paperwork. While we aren't sure that it is very meaningful when applied to him, we do not really object to it.

We went over the provisions about being able to leave the room—an accommodation he was using less and less, we wrote, but "it is comforting to him to know it is there." We mentioned the medication and what we had been doing to encourage socialization, including the camps and the Gay Center.

And we closed with a strong request that every teacher pay attention to the principles laid out in the IEP. Good things have been happening for Joseph in school, we wrote, "but they wouldn't be happening if not for the IEP and the vigilant attention everyone has paid to making sure it reflects Joseph's needs and is fully implemented."

We seemed to finally be getting the hang of this advocacy thing.

CHAPTER TWELVE

For all of the problems kids like Joseph might have, it's an amazing time to be L, G, B, or T in America. Culture and attitudes are growing more supportive all the time, and the legal landscape is shifting at an astonishing rate.

America is, very simply, growing to be more accepting of gay life and gay rights.

Let's start with the numbers. When the Gallup organization asked Americans, "Do you personally believe gay or lesbian relations are morally acceptable or morally wrong?" in 2001, just 40 percent said "morally acceptable," and 53 percent said "morally wrong." By 2011, the numbers had reversed: 56 percent were on the side of "morally acceptable," and 39 percent said "morally wrong." The same "values and beliefs" poll by Gallup found for the first time that a majority of Americans support same-sex marriage, having risen from 27 percent in 1996 to 53 percent in 2011.

Demographics suggest that this support is only likely to grow over time: of those polled between the ages of eighteen and thirty-four there was 70 percent support for same-sex marriage. Among those fifty-five and older, the support figure was just 39 percent. Intolerance is aging out.

Even the careful language of the Gallup pollsters had a ring of the momentous. "Americans are now as accepting of gays and lesbians as at any point in the last three decades, if not in U.S. history," the company reported. "This greater acceptance extends to their views of the morality of gay and lesbian relations, of their legality, and of whether marriage should legally be granted to same-sex couples."

That shift in national attitude is matched by a gradual broadening of acceptance in popular culture. On television, it's not just that there's a lovable gay character like Kurt on *Glee*. Popular culture increasingly treats gay people as part of life's banquet, part of any ensemble cast. It even predates the popular NBC sitcom *Will & Grace*, which ran from 1998 to 2006. A history in 2002 in *USA Today* discussed dozens of gay characters on television over the years, including Ellen DeGeneres, who came out as a lesbian on her sitcom, *Ellen*, and in real life in 1997.[79] The depiction of sympathetic gay characters goes all the way back to 1971, when Archie Bunker had a friend who turned out to be gay on *All in the Family*.

Being outed used to end Hollywood careers, but not anymore. DeGeneres's sitcom was cancelled a year after she came out, but she went on to create a blazingly successful daytime talk show. Neil Patrick Harris can be happily out and boast about his twins on his Twitter feed, all the while playing a straight lothario on *How I Met Your Mother*.

For years, Hollywood went along with the nation's homophobia, says Vito Russo in his study *The Celluloid Closet: Homosexuality in the Movies.*[80] Early films showed gay men as "frivolous, asexual sissies" even before the Production Code made sympathetic portrayals of homosexuality taboo. These days, a film like *Brokeback Mountain*, a story of two cowboys' long romantic relationship, can find a huge audience and win big at the Academy Awards and Golden Globes.

Acceptance has spread to other media as well. Archie, Betty, and Veronica now have a gay classmate, Kevin Keller.[81] In September 2011, the publisher announced that Kevin would be marrying another man.[82]

Of course, these changes have come with a backlash. In fact, the more that acceptance of gay sexual orientation grows, the fiercer that backlash has become. Politically, it is a largely conservative phenomenon: Democrats were more likely to be supportive of the morality of gay relations and same-sex marriage than Republicans, and liberals more supportive than conservatives.

Antigay groups and activists reliably speak out against even the most seemingly trivial cultural phenomena—remember that evangelist Jerry Falwell once attacked the children's show *Teletubbies* for its purple, bag-carrying character Tinky-Winky, saying, "As a Christian I feel that role modeling the gay lifestyle is damaging to the moral lives of children."[83] There was Peter Sprigg, a senior fellow at the Family Research Council, commenting on the Kevin Keller announcement:[84] "It's unfortunate that a comic book series usually seen as depicting innocent, all-American life is now being used to advance the sexual revolution." Kevin McCullough, a conservative columnist and radio host, criticized *Glee* on the conservative Townhall.com website for its depiction of two boys falling in love as delivering a "dangerous message," citing the elevated suicide rate among gay teens as evidence that gay sex is unsafe.[85] He wrote, "If the producers of *Glee* really claimed to 'love' homosexual males they would develop a story line where two boys were committed to each other but sexually abstinent for the sake of safety alone."

In attacking popular depictions of homosexuality, the conservative critics can be counted on to frame homosexuality as a lifestyle and a choice instead of the biological imperative that a growing body of scientific research shows it to be. The distinction is not important solely because of the moral message it sends: the Gallup poll showed that a person's view of the origins of sexual orientation is a major factor in one's likelihood to support gay rights, to an even greater extent than political leaning.

In fact, the pollster reported, "Americans' beliefs about the origins of same-sex orientation are much more strongly related to their views of the legality and morality of gay or lesbian relations than to party identification, ideology, religious commitment, age, and other demographic characteristics, taking all those factors into account simultaneously."

That understanding of the biological nature of sexual orientation is growing. With the rise in Americans' belief that homosexuality is a product of biology instead of upbringing comes greater acceptance. As I mentioned earlier, the 2011 Gallup survey showed that 40 percent of Americans say that being gay or lesbian is "something a person is born with," up from 13 percent in 1978. That has a practical effect on other attitudes: 81 percent of those who believe sexual orientation is biological in origin told Gallup that gay and lesbian relations are morally acceptable, as opposed to 33 percent of those who say that environment is the cause. When the subject is the legality of gay and lesbian relations, a whopping 87 percent of those who believe that sexual orientation is biological in origin told Gallup that "Gay/Lesbian relations should be legal," as opposed to 43 percent of those who say that environment is the cause.

In other words, the more someone believes that a person doesn't really have a lot of choice about sexual orientation, the more they support gay rights. A very religious person might say "that's the way God made him," instead of citing a string of studies, but the belief in the immutability of sexual attraction and the consequent lack of moral blame is the same. People who say they know a gay person also tend to be more supportive of gay rights than those who say they do not—and so the greater willingness of people to come out to friends and family can have a powerful effect.[86]

Support for the notion that biology is the origin of sexual orientation has been aided by the march of science and news coverage that has captured the public's imagination.

Sometimes, a single article in a newspaper can make a difference. Like the story of the gay penguins.

Now, newspaper reporters are people with an eye for unusual facts. Let's face it; it's more of an obsession, just as getting into journalism is more a compulsive disorder than a career.

We live for the moment when we know something other people don't—something that we can tell everybody, that will knock them back. So at a place like the *Times*, gathering at the lunch table is a daily opportunity to test each other, a combination of *Jeopardy!* and the *Thousand and One Nights*.

One day in 2004, Dinitia Smith, a worldly wise reporter

who was then working in the culture section, excitedly talked about the story she was working on: gay penguins. It wasn't a story from the news—the we've-gotta-write-it-because-the-president-said-it kind of thing. This was that rarer and lovelier thing: the conceptual scoop. The thing that makes your editor raise his eyebrows, show a manic smile, and say, "We've gotta get this in the paper!"

That's the kind of story Dinitia had. She'd found Roy and Silo, two chinstrap penguins at the Central Park Zoo in New York City who bonded six years before. They had even become loving parents, she wrote: "At one time, the two seemed so desperate to incubate an egg together that they put a rock in their nest and sat on it, keeping it warm in the folds of their abdomens." When their keeper gave them a fertile egg, "Roy and Silo sat on it for the typical thirty-four days until a chick, Tango, was born."

In the story, "The love that dare not squeak its name," she riffed with admirable agility on the broader subject of homosexual relations in the animal kingdom.[87] She cited Bruce Bagemihl, who published *Biological Exuberance: Animal Homosexuality and Natural Diversity* in 1999 and had documented homosexual behavior in hundreds of species.

Dinitia also cited Marlene Zuk, a professor of biology at the University of California at Riverside and author of *Sexual Selections: What We Can and Can't Learn About Sex from Animals*. Zuk noted that scientists have speculated that homosexuality may have an evolutionary purpose, ensuring the survival of the species. By not producing their own offspring, homosexuals may help support or nurture their relatives' young. "That is a contribution to the gene pool," she said.

But Zuk also warned against reading too much into animal behavior, noting that infanticide is widespread in the animal kingdom, too. "We shouldn't be using animals to craft moral and social policies for the kinds of human societies we want to live in. Animals don't take care of the elderly. I don't particularly think that should be a platform for closing down nursing homes."

Still, the broader message that biology has a lot to do with sexual orientation had been nudged forward and placed in a nonthreatening context of adorableness.

Dinitia was not the first to note the phenomenon of animals that did not mate boy-girl—or even the first story about gay penguins, for that matter. There was a lovely piece in the online magazine *Salon* in 2002 about Wendell and Cass, an Emperor penguin couple at the New York Aquarium.[88] But the front page of the *New York Times* reaches millions and helped give the ideas underlying the piece a long-lived resonance.

The idea that gay penguins can say something about same-sex attraction and biology came up again when *March of the Penguins* became a hit in 2005. Andrew Sullivan in London's *Sunday Times* wrote that while the film was championed by conservatives and Christian groups as affirming stable family relationships, penguin life was more complicated than the movie's fans might realize.

As he put it, "Some penguins are—wait for it—gay. Of course, any fool could have told you that. They're invariably impeccably turned out, in simple and elegant black tie with a very discrete splash of colour, and you can't tell the boys from the girls. This is a big problem for zoos hoping for baby penguins. The keepers at Berlin's Bremerhaven zoo were frustrated for years wondering why their penguin couples weren't producing any eggs. After DNA testing they discovered that three of the five pairs had the avian equivalent of 'civil partnerships.'"

The penguins had become a parable, one that said to millions of people who might not ponder a technical study or activist manifesto, "This is natural. This is part of life." A children's book about Silo and Roy, *And Tango Makes Three*, appeared in 2005.[89]

The existence of gay animals so strongly suggests that sexual orientation is largely based on biology—and normal—that the American Psychological Association and other groups cited Bagemihl's *Biological Exuberance* in a 2003 brief for the Supreme Court.[90] The case was a challenge to Texas's antisodomy law, which we'll be discussing in a bit.

Animals and homosexuality, of course, can be as controversial as anything having to do with human sexuality. My own contribution to the ongoing discussion appeared in 2007, when I wrote a front-page story for the *New York Times* about gay sheep.[91] The story discussed attacks on the work of a researcher at Oregon Health and Science University who was looking within the brain structure and chemistry for the physiological factors that make 8 percent of rams look to other rams (as opposed to ewes).

The activists at People for the Ethical Treatment of Animals launched a campaign against the research, accusing the lead scientist of trying to figure out how to "cure" gay sheep, an accusation that was trumpeted in London's *Sunday Times*.

It wasn't true, but it got a lot of attention—what, in the story, I referred to as "a textbook example of the distortion and vituperation that can result when science meets the global news cycle." Headline writers inevitably smirked. "Ewe Turn for Gay Rams on Hormones," one paper wrote. Another put it: "He's Just Not That Into Ewe."

On the one hand, the research supported the growing body of scientific evidence that suggested sexual orientation was controlled by biology, not environment. But the darker implications of that argument were just below the surface and exploited by PETA. As the *Sunday Times* put it, the research "could pave the way for breeding out homosexuality in humans" through hormone treatment or even abortion, as many parents now do with Down syndrome or Tay-Sachs disease.

That chilling outcome wasn't likely to happen and wasn't even the point of the research. But the fearmongering was used effectively by PETA.

Andrew Sullivan, who is gay, addressed the controversy simply[92] in his online column, saying "we should not fear such research but encourage more of it. As for PETA, I'm a defender of animal rights—but not their tactics in raising awareness" at least in this case.

As momentous as the changes in the cultural landscape have been, the shift in the American legal system in recent years may be even more impressive. Laws that classify homosexual acts as illegal have fallen, and laws that discriminated against gay people are under attack; laws that give LGBT people the same rights as their straight counterparts are on the move. It is an amazing time.

Many books have been written and will be written about each of the issues I'm about to discuss, but this tour of the horizon should drive home just how much is going on, and how quickly things are changing.

If there's one Supreme Court case to know the name of in this context, it's *Lawrence v. Texas*, the 2003 decision that struck down sodomy laws across the nation.[93]

The case involved the arrest of two men in Houston. Police responded to a false report of a disturbance and entered the apartment of John Geddes Lawrence, who according to police reports was having sex with Tyron Garner. The police arrested the two men for "deviate sexual intercourse," and a conviction followed. The case went up to the Supreme Court, which voted 6-3 to overturn Texas's law on the grounds that it violated the equal protection guarantees under the Fourteenth Amendment to penalize people for engaging in "certain intimate sexual conduct."

The decision overturned *Bowers v. Hardwick*, which had upheld Georgia's sodomy law in 1986. Now, with *Lawrence,* the court swept away sodomy laws in the thirteen other states that still made homosexual acts a criminal matter. "*Bowers* was not correct when it was decided, and it is not correct today," wrote Justice Anthony Kennedy in the majority opinion.

Justice Kennedy's language was simple, straightforward, and strong. "The petitioners are entitled to respect for their private lives. The State cannot demean their existence or control their destiny by making their private sexual conduct a crime."

Those who wrote the Constitution and the Fourteenth Amendment had created a document with the flexibility to extend its "components of liberty" into areas they may not have understood at the time, he wrote. "They knew times can blind us to certain truths and later generations can see that laws once thought necessary and proper in fact serve only to oppress. As the Constitution endures, persons in every generation can invoke its principles in their own search for greater freedom."

Lawrence is a monumental decision, the kind of thoughtful application of fundamental principles of freedom that proves the Constitution is an ongoing test of the nation's will.

This time, we passed.

Not everyone agrees, including three members of the Supreme Court. Justice Antonin Scalia wrote a scathing dissent in *Lawrence* that said the majority view "largely signed on to the so-called homosexual agenda. . . ." He insisted "I have nothing against homosexuals," but said that "the court has taken sides in the culture war, departing from its role of assuring, as neutral observer, that the democratic rules of engagement are observed."

He called up a litany of horrors, state laws that Justice Kennedy's opinion might ultimately overturn, including "bigamy, same-sex marriage, adult incest, prostitution, masturbation, adultery, fornication, bestiality, and obscenity." Such laws are only sustainable, he said, under the ability of the nation to base laws on moral choices, as the court had allowed in *Bowers*.

"Every single one of these laws is called into question by today's decision," Justice Scalia wrote. "This effectively decrees the end of all morals legislation."

Justice Kennedy's majority opinion mildly deflected the argument: "The present case does not involve minors. It does not involve persons who might be injured or coerced or who are situated in relationships where consent might not easily be refused. It does not involve public conduct or prostitution," he wrote.

And, specifically countering the same-sex marriage argument, he wrote, "It does not involve whether the government must give formal recognition to any relationship that homosexual persons seek to enter."

Well, maybe.

In the years since *Lawrence*, the case has been cited repeatedly to expand LGBT rights, along with *Romer v. Evans*, a 1996 decision also written by Justice Kennedy.[94] That case struck down a Colorado law that banned antidiscrimination laws specifically protecting gay people.

When the supreme court of Massachusetts legalized same-sex marriage in 2004, it cited *Lawrence*. So did United States District Judge Vaughn Walker in his 2010 decision overturning Proposition 8, California's ban on same-sex marriage.[95]

Same-sex marriage has emerged as one of the defining gay rights issues and a flashpoint in the nation's culture war. The California decision could turn out to be the key case. Proponents of the right to marry for same-sex couples argue that the principle is as fundamental a principle as that underlying the Supreme Court's decision in *Loving v. Virginia*, the case that struck down laws banning interracial marriage. Many supporters also say partial measures like domestic partnerships do not provide the range of benefits for couples that marriage provides automatically, from tax advantages to rights in inheritance and even access to a spouse in the hospital.

Opponents of gay marriage pose a moral argument that ultimately comes down to the prohibition in Leviticus, and claim that same-sex marriage undermines the institution of marriage.

At this writing, six states—along with Massachusetts, there's Connecticut, Iowa, Vermont, New Hampshire and New York, and the District of Columbia as well—allow same-sex marriage.[96] Thirty-seven states have laws defining marriage as being between a man and a woman, and thirty states have constitutional amendments to that effect.

And then there's California, which was for gay marriage before it was against it. In May 2008, the state's supreme court overturned a voter initiative from eight years before that stated only marriages between a man and a woman would be recognized by the state.

The floodgates opened. Over the next few months, 18,000 couples got marriage licenses. But by the next election in November 2008, opponents of same-sex marriage had a new initiative on the ballot—terse enough to fit in a Tweet—that declared: "Only marriage between a man and a woman is valid or recognized in California." That initiative passed narrowly, and the floodgates slammed shut again.

When an attempt to overturn Prop 8 reached the California Supreme Court, the justices decided, essentially, that the initiative process was more important than the right to use the word "marriage" to describe a civil union, and let the law stand.

That's when a new legal challenge at the federal level began, with two star lawyers, David Boies and Theodore Olson, running the case. [97] They had stood on opposite sides in the battle over the Florida recount in the 2000 presidential election, but they were united in fighting for the right of same-sex couples to marry. Olson is a conservative icon but told *New York Times* reporter Jo Becker that this case transcends political stereotypes and "could involve the rights and happiness and equal treatment of millions of people." [98]

Judge Walker wrote a forceful, densely reasoned opinion that cited *Lawrence* and quoted extensively from Ilan Meyer's testimony about minority stress, writing, "Meyer explained that Proposition 8 stigmatizes gays and lesbians because it informs gays and lesbians that the State of California rejects their relationships as less valuable than opposite-sex relationships. Proposition 8 also provides state endorsement of private discrimination. According to Meyer, Proposition 8 increases the likelihood of negative mental and physical health outcomes for gays and lesbians." The Ninth Circuit Court of Appeals upheld Judge Walker's decision in February 2012.

Making a federal case of same-sex marriage was a risky move, and controversial within the community of gay legal activists, who had been pursuing a more gradual, state-by-state approach. If the case gets to the Supreme Court and Boies and Olson lose, they fret that it will set back the movement. If they win, the upside is that the decision might allow same-sex marriage nationwide. But the possible downside is the kind of backlash that the Supreme Court's landmark abortion decision, *Roe v. Wade*, had. A libertarian legal scholar, Richard Epstein, told me for a story on shifts in jurisprudence over LGBT rights that "it would be terrible if this were like the abortion cases, and for the next forty years you were fighting a rear-guard action."[99]

The potential for backlash is real. After Iowa's supreme court unanimously approved same-sex marriage, voters removed three of the justices from office in a campaign led by opponents of gay marriage.

In any case, before long, Proposition 8 is probably going to be before the Supreme Court of the United States. What will Justice Kennedy do then?

In my mind's eye, I see the robed ones in their weekly judicial conference. And I see Justice Kennedy turning to Justice Scalia. With a twinkle in his eye, he says:

"Gee, Nino—I guess you were right!"

Does the fact that I have a gay son and write about these legal disputes mean that I'm biased—that my stories for the *New York Times* have been slanted? It's the kind of argument that I could expect people to make as part of the general attack these days on the so-called liberal media.

In a word, no. It does mean I do have opinions, but all journalists have opinions. The work of a journalist is not to bleach his brain of opinions and life experiences, but to write fairly in light of all available information. And that is what I have always done. I'd be happy to compare my coverage to anyone else's.

This does not mean that my stories give equal weight to every side of an argument, however; I'm no believer in false balance. In my years of science reporting, I came to understand that giving equal weight to the side of a scientific argument that didn't have actual science on its side was bad journalism, not fair journalism.

Take the long-running debate over evolution versus alternatives with names like creationism or intelligent design. The people promoting these alternatives to evolution deserve respect, and their arguments deserve to be heard, especially in legitimate news stories about their efforts in court to change science curriculums. What fairness calls for, however, is a proper examination of those efforts and the views underlying them, and a sober evaluation of the evidence they present. In a scientific conflict over evolution, it is important to note that the intelligent design folks are ultimately making a religious argument, not a scientific one; the paucity of their evidence stands up poorly against the robust mountains of evidence built by Darwin and those who came after. Faith must be respected, but its place is at church and in the home, not science class. My colleague Cornelia Dean, who writes extensively and compassionately about the conflict over evolution, consistently writes a line much like this one into her stories: "There is no credible scientific challenge to the theory of evolution as an explanation for the complexity and diversity of life on earth."[100]

I faced similar challenges when I covered tobacco as a science reporter at the *Washington Post*. The industry had spent years, and millions of dollars, trying to sow doubt as to whether smoking causes cancer. I wrote story after story about the tobacco wars of the 1990s, but I always pointed out that the evidence that smoking causes cancer is as solid as can be, with a seventeenfold increase in cancer risk for smokers. Tobacco executives and lobbyists praised my stories for their fairness, and thanked me for so carefully reporting the legal side of their legal arguments against the Food and Drug Administration efforts to regulate them. But fairness didn't require me to suggest that their products are safe.

In the battles over same-sex marriage, I brought the same overarching view: show me the evidence. As I went over the amicus briefs and testimony in the Prop 8 case, it became obvious that while the opponents of same-sex marriage had dressed up their moral argument as a scientific and legal one, they had no actual evidence that same-sex marriage harmed children or threatened conventional marriage.

When Judge Walker's opinion in the case came out, it contained a densely argued, point-by-point refutation of the pseudoscientific arguments made by same-sex marriage opponents. And, reading it with the eye of a science writer, I couldn't help but think that he got it right.

Judge Walker, by the way, is gay. Did that make him a biased judge? Once they had lost their case, the Proposition 8 supporters made that argument: They filed briefs demanding that Judge Walker's opinion be vacated on bias grounds. He should have recused himself from hearing the case, they said, because of his inherent bias. They argued that Judge Walker is not only gay—a fact that was known, if not discussed by the judge himself, during the trial—but that he acknowledged in an interview after the trial that he is in a long-term relationship himself. The briefs calling for vacating the opinion suggested that this meant that he could benefit personally from his decision, and thus was biased.

Like journalists, judges are not blank slates. They have lives, and they have opinions. At the time the challenge first came up, I wrote a story that quoted Monroe H. Freedman, an expert in legal ethics at Hofstra Law School. He said that while bias could lead to recusal in rare cases, "you could say, 'If a gay judge is disqualified, how about a straight judge?' There isn't anybody about whom somebody might say, 'You're not truly impartial in this case.'"[101]

He told me about a 1975 opinion by Judge Constance Baker Motley of Federal District Court. She is black, and had been asked to disqualify herself from a discrimination suit. "If background or sex or race of each judge were, by definition, sufficient grounds for removal, no judge on this court could hear this case, or many others," she wrote.

The first judge to hear the argument about throwing out Judge Walker's opinion on bias grounds wrote that the claim that Judge Walker might some day want to marry his partner was far too speculative to establish bias. The idea that a gay judge couldn't adjudicate a gay issue, he wrote, "is as warrantless as the presumption that a female judge is incapable of being impartial in a case in which women seek legal relief."

That opinion was appealed, and when the case was heard at the Ninth Circuit Court of Appeals, one of the three judges on the panel, N. Randy Smith, asked the lead attorney for the opponents of same-sex marriage, "So a married judge could never hear a divorce?" Smith is one of the most conservative members of the circuit, appointed by President George W. Bush. But he knows the law, and his question suggests that he knows a sour grapes argument when he hears one.

Is it biased of me to think that? I'd call it an informed opinion.

And by the way, the Ninth Circuit didn't buy the argument, either.

Another law that restricts the rights of same-sex couples is also under attack, though it gets less attention than Proposition 8. The Defense of Marriage Act, which was passed during the Clinton administration in 1996, prohibits the federal government from recognizing same-sex marriage.

That law, over time, has hit many couples hard. When Edith S. Windsor of New York lost her spouse, Thea C. Spyer, in 2009, their Canadian marriage was recognized by New York State.[102] But Ms. Windsor ran into trouble with federal tax laws. If the two had been a man and a woman, there would have been no federal estate tax to pay. Because of DOMA, Ms. Windsor owed the government $350,000. She sued, as part of a case launched by the American Civil Liberties Union. When I wrote about the case, Ms. Windsor told me that she had been the youngest child in her family and had always been blamed for things. It left an impression. "I care about justice," she said, "and this is so unjust."[103]

The new case, and another one involving couples in Connecticut that was spearheaded by the group Gay & Lesbian Advocates & Defenders, put the Obama administration in a difficult position.

Barack Obama had run for president saying that he favored gay rights and opposed the Defense of Marriage Act, even though he said he was not personally in favor of gay marriage. He said, however, that his view on gay marriage was "evolving."

In the Defense of Marriage Act cases, however, the Department of Justice defended the law's constitutionality. When pressed, Justice Department officials would say that the executive branch historically defends laws passed by Congress as presumptively constitutional.

It was a frustrating answer for supporters of same-sex marriage, especially after a federal judge in Massachusetts declared the law unconstitutional in 2010.[104]

In February 2011, the Department of Justice dropped a bombshell by announcing that it would no longer defend DOMA as constitutional.[105] [106] Supporters of the law in Congress then allocated money to hire attorneys who are carrying on the defense of the law.

If those legal battles aren't enough, recent years have also seen a rancorous fight over repealing the policy known as "Don't Ask, Don't Tell," which prohibited openly gay or bisexual people from serving in the military. As a candidate for president, Obama pledged to end it, but—again—his Justice Department defended it in court in its traditional role.

Obama urged Congress to repeal the law. Congress did vote to repeal the seventeen-year-old policy in 2010 after a federal judge in California declared that it, too, was unconstitutional.[107] The next year, the branches of the military completed the steps necessary under the law to finally end "Don't Ask, Don't Tell."

With so much change for the rights of gay, lesbian, bisexual, and transgendered people coming through the federal courts, I wrote an essay in September 2010 that asked whether federal judges were becoming increasingly willing to strike down what they see as antigay bias embodied in legislation. Erwin Chemerinsky, the law school dean at the University of California, Irvine, answered me this way: "Federal judges are no longer persuaded that a moral condemnation of homosexuality justifies government discrimination."[108]

Meanwhile, Barack Obama's evolution continued. On May 9, 2012, he said the words that millions of people had hoped to hear: "I think same-sex couples should be able to get married."[109]

The fight over issues like same-sex marriage might seem symbolic to outside observers. Gay friends have quietly confided to me that they don't care whether same-sex couples can *really* marry, and even more quietly wonder whether it has been a good idea to expend so much political capital on a topic that engenders such bitter pushback from conservative religious and political groups.

Charles Kaiser, a reporter and author of *The Gay Metropolis*, a phenomenal history of gay life in America, explained it to me this way: "I'm a skeptic, but not because of the right-wing pushback," he said. "I just don't think that being openly and proudly gay means that we should be as much like straight people as possible." Seeking marriage always seemed to him like an attempt at imitation, he said; "the whole point of being gay is to be different—to form our own kinds of relationships and bonds."

That isn't the way Rich Meislin feels, however. Rich and his partner, Hendrik Uyttendaele, a dermatologist born in Belgium, got married at their house in the Catskills in October 2011. New York had, just that summer, approved same-sex marriage, and they realized that for their twentieth anniversary together they wanted to wed.

With their friends there to celebrate and before exchanging vows, Rich and Hendrik explained, as they put it, "why we're doing this," reading alternating passages of a gentle essay that they wrote together.

"In our own eyes, and in our hearts, we have already been married for twenty years," Rich said.

Hendrik then talked about their shared love of their mountain house and eclectic musical tastes that range from jazz to Cuban hip-hop, of travel and cooking, "And best of all, we share a tremendous reservoir of love that has grown as the years have passed."

Rich then said, "What we don't share is a legal bond. But who cares?" They hadn't bothered to become domestic partners, and the likelihood that they would have the much-publicized problems of nonmarried partners under the law—things like not being able to automatically take over each other's hypothetical food-cart licenses—"were pretty low."

The intensity of the fight over changing New York's law, Hendrik responded, made it clear that there was still much to be done. "To our minds, now that it has been seized, this right has to be used." Their marriage was a bond of love, then, but also a political act and a message.

"Every marriage of two men or two women moves things a little closer for those who don't have the right in their own states today," Hendrik said, "and for the still-unwon battle for equality under federal law."

Rich added that "people have long since realized that the simple act of coming out can change others' views of gay people. It's harder to simultaneously hold the thoughts that you hate generic gay people, but you like Hendrik, or you like Rich."

And so, he concluded, "We're hoping that our marriage today, even though it's just one marriage, can also help change people's views. Gay marriage threatens the institution of marriage? Your marriage is threatened? By Hendrik? By Rich? Really?"

Charles Kaiser, a longtime friend of Rich, attended the wedding. After the ceremony, Rich recalled, Charles came up to them and said, "You convinced me."

In our conversation, Charles told me that he still counts himself among the skeptics, though he was moved by the ceremony. "I was never a big advocate of 'everyone should get married,' though obviously I believe everyone should have *the right* to be married—that everyone should be able to make this choice without the government having any role in it." For himself and his partner, he said, he is still waiting for the moment when same-sex marriage becomes truly equal to the heterosexual variety in the eyes of the federal government, after the

Defense of Marriage Act is repealed by Congress, or thrown out by the United States Supreme Court.

Still, the wedding brought him a new understanding, he said. "Their vows were so moving, and so beautiful, that I realized that for some people, getting married would have exactly the same desirable effect that it had for successful heterosexual marriages—mainly, deepening and clarifying the reasons two people have chosen to share their lives together.

"Their vows did that," he said, "as elegantly and as movingly as anything I've ever heard."

Rich and Hendrik's wedding, and all the others, help heal the damage done by laws like Proposition 8; they help correct the impression that, as Ilan Meyer put it in describing the law's impact on gay people, "I'm really not seen as equal."

Judge Stephen Reinhardt of the Court of Appeals of the Ninth Circuit, in upholding Judge Walker's decision, wrote that the supporters of Proposition 8 had not provided evidence that justified the law. The state's same-sex marriage ban, he wrote, "serves no purpose, and has no effect, other than to lessen the status and human dignity of gays and lesbians in California, and to officially reclassify their relationships and families as inferior to those of opposite-sex couples."[110]

Judge Reinhardt argued that words matter. "If Marilyn Monroe's film had been named *How to Register a Domestic Partnership with a Millionaire*," then "it would not have conveyed the same meaning. . . ." And so, he wrote, "the name 'marriage' signifies the unique recognition that society gives to harmonious, loyal, enduring, and intimate relationships."

We don't know if Joseph Schwartz will ever want to get

married; Jeanne and I have straight friends who are happily single. But we don't want anybody telling our son that if he finds somebody that he wants to spend the rest of his life with someday, he's not good enough to call it a marriage.

Joseph's big sister, Elizabeth, tied the knot with her college sweetheart a couple of years ago in Austin. Joseph helped pick out her wedding dress and loved the ceremony, which took place on a perfect spring day at the Lady Bird Johnson Wildflower Center. Joseph was an usher and looked very grown-up in his suit. Since then, he has paid close attention to marriage fights in the states.

Joe, and kids like him, don't need to read Judge Reinhardt's opinion, or to study the research of Ilan Meyer, to know that laws like Proposition 8 say they are inferior.

And that it's not right.

CHAPTER THIRTEEN

Whether I shall turn out to be the hero of my own life, or whether that station will be held by anybody else, these pages must show.

—CHARLES DICKENS, *DAVID COPPERFIELD*

High school, for many of us, is the chance for a fresh start that sets us on the path to the grown-up we're going to be. It is where we try on personalities to see what fits. I had written an essay for the *Times* a couple of years before Joe got to high school about the fact that his older brother, Sam, wore a brightly colored poncho to school on Fridays.[111] In no time, it became his trademark, with some razzing and some irritation from coaches and fellow students along the way. Toward the end of the essay, I shifted from a generally comic tone to a more serious thought:

Defining yourself is the central question of adolescence. We ask, Am I a jock or a geek? A joker or a hippie? Am I smart? Good looking? Am I enough like everyone else? Am I distinctive? We are pulled in every direction. Sam has asked the question and, I think, begun to answer it well.

Now it is Joe's time to answer the question. At an age when kids look for their labels, Joseph has found one: he is the gay kid. He began attending meetings of the school's gay-straight alliance in ninth grade and encouraged other kids to come with him into Manhattan for functions at the Gay Center.

Joseph seized this new identity with a playful ease. After he had earned a nonspeaking part in the school's fall musical, Jeanne told me the other kids in the show called him "G.A.C.," pronounced "Gack." When Jeanne asked him why, Joseph explained that at the first rehearsal, the cast members were asked to go around the room and state their name, grade, and one thing about themselves.

When it was his turn, my son said this:

"I'm Joseph Schwartz, I'm in ninth grade, and I'm gay as Christmas."

We had never heard the expression before, but Joe explained that he had picked up the phrase the previous summer, at French Woods. A much-loved counselor, the woman who taught the stage-fighting class, had used it.

A quick look at the Urban Dictionary website shows that it's common in, um, some circles. The site puts it this way: "An extremely over-the-top, overtly feminine gay man or teenage boy. Thought originally to be a reference to the Christmas carol 'Deck the Halls,' which contains the line: 'Don we now our gay apparel.'"[112]

To our relief, the high school turned out to be a surprisingly welcoming place that took the fight against bullying seriously, and even started the school year with an assembly on the topic. Several years before, the state had passed one of the strongest anti-bullying laws in the nation.

Bullying and anti-gay prejudice simply weren't tolerated. Jason, our daughter Elizabeth's gay friend, told me about having been insulted when he began ninth grade a few years before. Jason was in the cafeteria line as it snaked through the lunchroom, and came up behind some kids at a table. One of the boys at the table said to the other, "You better watch your back, because the kid behind you is a fag." Jason marched over to the vice principal's office to report the incident.

"The guy who was standing with me backed me up," Jason recalled, and the other kids at the table acknowledged what had been said. The principal suspended the boy, and Jason recalled, "I ended up quite smug about it."

For his part, Joseph began to find allies in surprising places. The school nurse at the high school pays close attention to him, and urged him to come see her whenever he feels his emotions are getting out of hand or if he feels unwell.

The nurse stepped in after Joseph had spells of light-headedness after PE class. She took it on as a physical, not a psychological, issue and suggested that Jeanne include more protein in Joe's lunch and a quick snack before gym, like peanut-butter crackers. Jeanne followed her advice, and Joseph reported feeling much better. The nurse was teaching him an important lesson: your problems might not be in your head. Simple changes in your habits can have an effect on your mood and well-being.

The nature of exercise was different at the high school as well. The PE department offered a range of classes instead of the one-size-fits-all approach of middle school. Jocks could focus on sports, while kids like Joe could choose classes in dance and yoga, where you never get picked last. It was liberating.

In those and so many other ways, Joseph had come into a school that was ready to support him. Tyler Clementi's suicide, which occurred just after Joseph started ninth grade, raised the level of sensitivity even higher.

Meanwhile, Joseph was finding that for all he had been through, things were much worse for other gay kids he knew. During his weekly sessions at the Center, at the camp, and even within our suburban GSA, Joe's friends had opened his eyes by talking about the problems and personal crises they have suffered. He heard about the struggles of transgender kids, who had to deal with society's rejection, who have to consider issues like hormone treatments and surgery, and for whom even pronouns are tricky. At first, the stories were so intense that Joseph would have to quietly leave the room to calm down, but over time he learned to stay, to listen. To learn.

Joseph got the message. His friends' experiences have given him a better outlook on his own, and he now says, "My backstory is pretty mild."

So much attention at school had been devoted to identifying Joseph as a kid with problems that it was easy to lose perspective, to think that his situation was especially dire. The Center's YES program was a lesson in perspective—not just for Joe but for us. We met with one of the Center counselors before sending Joseph off to camp that first time. We wanted to warn him about our son's emotional outbursts, his fragility; we told him that we didn't want him to be surprised to find that he was dealing with a boy who has problems.

"Look around you," he said. "We all have problems. This is a community that has a *lot* of problems."

As spring of his freshman year rolled around, Joseph decided to act on something he had been thinking about since he had been to camp with the kids from YES. A counselor whose hair color seemed to change by the week had suggested that Joseph might want to dye his hair. Joseph first mentioned this desire to Jeanne at the end of the summer. Jeanne initially put him off, telling him to ease into the new environment and test the waters first. By the spring, though, Joseph was insistent. He was doing reasonably well in school; teachers had learned to say to their classes, "Okay, let's hear the answer from somebody *other* than Joseph." This time, Jeanne thought that the request was serious enough that we should discuss it as a family. So, one evening in March, Joseph told me, "I really want to dye my hair purple."

When he was little, Joseph had wanted to paint his room purple. It had always been his favorite color. But on his head? I didn't try to argue him out of it; dye, unlike a tattoo, isn't permanent. But I did want him to consider the possible consequences.

"You know, Joe, there is a pretty significant possibility that you will get pounded at school." He said that he understood but told me he didn't really think that would happen.

I called around to the local hair salons; none of them said they could do a purple dye job. So I decided that on Saturday, we'd head over to Astor Place Hairstylists, the venerable salon in the East Village. They've been cutting, fading, and dyeing since 1947. It's a place that has always been up for anything.

So on a chilly Saturday in March after Joseph finished up at the Gay Center, we walked over to Astor Place. The colorist, however, tried to talk Joseph out of his purple idea. "Purple is for ladies," she said. "It's not a good color for a boy." She recommended blue. Joseph agreed, and she set to work applying the peroxide that would bleach his dark brown hair enough to take the dye.

As his hair was going to yellowish white—and Joseph's scalp was burning from the harsh chemicals—he decided to dig in. He got up and told the colorist, "I really want the purple." She nodded and got out two small jars of dye. After a couple of hours (and about a hundred bucks, with the very nice haircut thrown in), his hair was an eye-popping shade of purple.

We drove back across the Hudson, and Joseph reminded me that he wanted to attend the school dramatic performance that evening. I walked him into the school to buy the ticket and saw the principal from across the entryway. And the principal saw Joseph. His eyes got pretty big. I couldn't read his facial expression, but if I were to guess, it was one of self-pity—as in, "I'm going to be dealing with this on Monday. This kid is going to get picked on, and it's going to end up in my office."

I went home and posted a few pictures to Facebook with the caption, "Joseph Schwartz has decided to see what life is like with purple hair for a while. . . ."

My brother Bob, who is bald, wrote, "I am jealous."

A friend who is a professor at a top-ranked law school wrote, "Buy black towels and pillowcases. I speak from experience here." I waited nervously for something bad to happen, but disaster never came. Purple hair was Joe's version of Sam's poncho: bright and attention getting, but ultimately part of his school persona.

Still, not all of the attention was friendly. A few days after going purple, Joseph was in the locker room after gym when one of the jocks came up to him and asked, "Why did you dye your hair purple?"

Joseph said, "Because it's awesome."

The other boy didn't accept that answer. "Yeah, but—Why didn't you dye it orange, or something?"

"Because orange would not look good with my coloring," Joseph explained.

The kid became even more insistent and pulled out some of the high-dollar vocabulary words from SAT prep: "But don't you understand—*don't you understand*—that the color purple has been appropriated by the homosexuals?"

A kid piped up from across the room, "He's really aware of that."

The jock responded, "I was just trying to warn him—"

At that point, another of the jocks came up and slammed Jock #1 into a bank of lockers. "He can dye his hair hot fucking *pink* if he wants to," the boy shouted. "He can dye it any fucking color he wants!" The two boys walked out of the locker room, arguing with each other about Joe's hair. Joseph turned to the boy he shared a locker with and said, "That was surreal."

At the end of ninth grade, Joseph's psychiatrist made a surprising suggestion.

They had been seeing each other once every few months since the suicide attempt. During each visit, the doctor would ask Joseph questions to determine whether his depression was creeping back. The doctor was sensitive, and was obviously weighing what Joseph had to say about his recent experiences.

He didn't look for new diagnostic labels to stick on Joseph, and his attitude toward medication was conservative: he was reluctant to increase Joe's dosage, trying to see first if Joseph could find his own path to resolving issues of stress and pressure. We felt lucky to have found him.

On that day in May, he noted that it had been quite some time since Joseph had reported any problems to him. The doctor told us that it might be time to wean Joseph off the drug.

Jeanne and I were intrigued by the idea. We had friends whose kids had been put on one drug after another, with escalating doses and side effects. It was one of the things that had worried us about medication. We did have one concern, however: we were at the end of the school year. That had been the time that Joseph traditionally had the most stress and trouble in the past. I reached out to a friend in Massachusetts who is a psychiatrist, and she said the change made sense if the depression had eased. The drug might be helping to manage symptoms like impulsivity or regulation of his moods, she wrote, but "there are significant medical risks of long-term use." Considering our past conversations about Joseph, she concluded, "this is likely to be just fine."

We stopped the drug. After a few days of adjustment, Joseph seemed . . . just fine.

After six weeks, he went back to the psychiatrist's office for a follow-up visit.

"How are you feeling?" the doctor asked. "Any problems?"

"It's been good," Joseph answered, adding that there had been "a brief moment of existential dread today." There had been no panic attacks.

"If things are going well without medicine, there's no need

for medicine," the doctor said. The treatment was over, though he added, "The door here is open if you need it."

A lot was happening. But one thing was not happening yet: dating. The GSA was great, but it was made up almost entirely of girls. Joseph loved the kids at the Center but didn't feel a strong physical attraction to anyone he knew there. "When the hell am I going to have a boyfriend?" he'd ask. He knew that college would present new opportunities, but it was still years away. An eternity.

That summer, at French Woods, he had a brief relationship with a boy from across the country. It couldn't last; they'd agreed to break off at the end of camp and not try to have a long-distance relationship. But it was a start.

That summer also led to a great role onstage for Joseph: a speaking part in French Woods's production of *Spamalot*. The role is a common kind of character in the Monty Python canon: a man dressed as a woman. Joseph, his purple hair faded to silver, played the mother of Sir Galahad. He screeched his way across the stage, getting big laughs. He also had enormous breasts, having borrowed a brassiere from a friend and packed it with laundry.

A few weeks after getting home from French Woods, he ended the summer by heading back to gay camp. Just before that trip, he dyed his hair such a bright shade of red that the conductor on the train home asked him if he'd lost a bet.

I called my mom to tell her about the new color. She sensed so early that there was something different about Joe and had always dealt with his quirks with warmth and good humor.

When he came out, she was as relieved as we were, and she suffered through his time in the hospital.

"I'm proud of Joe," she said. "But I'm really proud of you two for being so supportive."

I told her that we couldn't have imagined it any other way. "We know how terrible things are if he can't be who he is," I explained. "And now he really is who he is.

"Boy, is he who he is," I said.

Summer was over. School started again; Joe was a sophomore. In September 2011, the year after the Clementi suicide, yet another antibullying law went into effect that was even tougher than the one that had been in place before. Known as the "Antibullying Bill of Rights," it is broadly considered the nation's toughest. The law requires schools to engage in extensive training of staff and students, and to appoint safety teams made up of parents, teachers, and staff. Each allegation of bullying required launching an immediate investigation. The law has been criticized for reaching too far into the private lives of students and creating new burdens for the schools without providing the resources to pay for meeting the new requirements.[113] But no one could doubt the state's seriousness in addressing the issue. *Time* magazine wrote, "New Jersey is putting itself out in front nationally on the issue of bullying—and standing firmly with the victims. That is the right place to be."[114]

The school hosted sessions for the kids, and an evening meeting for parents as well on the harassment, intimidation, and bullying program, known by the initials HIB. I decided to attend. The principal introduced the school district's antibullying coordinator, a role created by the new law. The coordinator explained that "bullying has changed." Kids can torment one another remotely, over the Internet, he said, and can gang up virtually to devastating effect. He wasn't saying it out loud, but it had not been long since the high school had been in the middle of a media storm over cyberbullying among high school girls, who tormented the new freshmen with mean "slam book" comments. Parents had complained, and the school had taken disciplinary measures.

The bullying coordinator acknowledged that some parents had asked him, "Can't we just let our kids be kids? Isn't this going a little over the top?" Yes, kids have to learn to deal with conflict if they are going to develop normally, he said, and there is still a common-sense difference between single incidents and patterns of harassment or bullying. It won't necessarily turn into a big deal "every time a kid pokes another kid," he explained.

"But if it happens repeatedly, if it's an ongoing problem, it could be found to be HIB."

Change is happening at the middle school as well. Folks there tell me that they are working toward starting a mini GSA. They plan to give it a name less likely to raise parental concerns—Diversity Club, anyone? Whatever they call it, we hope they get it off the ground. There are other kids like Joseph out there, and they need a posse.

As Joseph makes his way through the high school, some students have said he has become a kind of role model there. Several kids in recent months have chosen to come out to Joseph, and one girl a year younger than Joseph proudly told her dad, a friend of mine, that Joseph was her buddy, and that he was out.

The dad hadn't known that about Joe, and I'd never told

him. This was a guy who, when I had written a story about Proposition 8 the year before, had joked in a note to me "You know I love the fagelas." After his daughter's revelation, he wrote me another note that showed a different attitude. Being so open and honest about sexual orientation so young, he said, "is very rare" and shows "impressive maturity and ability to know thyself."

Then he joked, "I am a proponent of the unexamined life, being the only one worth living."

Clearly, as the strain of keeping a secret and feeling all alone eased, Joseph opened up socially. All those oopses and ouches in the Center group seem to be helping to sand off some of his rough edges. Our boy, once so gloomy, has become a smiler. During a crimson-haired phase, he wore a black T-shirt to school on the day of the weekly GSA meeting that sported a big rainbow and read "LGBTerrific!" After being told in middle school that a T-shirt saying "GAY" could cause trouble, we were a little nervous. But nothing happened. And somehow, he made that T-shirt look good.

For his sixteenth birthday, he asked for a party—just a trip to a good restaurant with friends, but after the Build-A-Bear disaster, it feels big.

All of this isn't to say that things are perfect. Stress continues to plague our son. He signed up for the school musical in the fall and, as the rehearsals and dance practices took up more and more of his day, felt himself falling behind in classes and sliding toward exhaustion. He broke down one day in the lunchroom and told the school psychologist that he felt depression edging back. Once he calmed down, he left her office and went to the drama teacher to drop out of the musical—a good sign, we felt, that he is trying to manage his own emotional landscape.

Meanwhile, we continue to work with the school on making sure Joseph gets the accommodations he needs, and that he doesn't have any that he doesn't need. His psychologist at school tells us that she marvels at the fact that we are always pressing to make Joe's IEP thinner. These days, most of what we really want is an understanding within the school of his emotional vulnerability, to get the extra time on tests, and to be able to use a laptop instead of having to force his balky fingers to use a pen or pencil.

"The other parents want more accommodations," they say. "They *sue* if they don't get them."

That's just not us. To many parents, advocacy does mean a lawsuit. Friends of ours have successfully sued the school district over provision of services, and know that litigation has been a key factor in moving rights and services forward. But while we've learned a lot about advocating for our child, we've also tried to learn when to step back.

We do wish it hadn't taken so long to learn those lessons. In elementary school, the game had seemed rigged and we were still clueless. Maybe we could have started yelling louder, sooner, and taken our complaints higher within the school district to get Joseph treated more humanely, and to have him freed from the worst teachers. By middle school and high school, it became easier to work with administrators and teachers to resolve problems.

Joseph, meanwhile, continues to grow—and I don't just mean that he towers over me. On any given afternoon nowadays, you can see him walking home deep in conversation with a friend, or sitting at the library with buddies, reading a novel while they study. We're hoping he will actually study with them at some point. He is in chorus and takes piano and voice lessons outside of school. He can sing Giacomo Carissimi's "Vittoria, mio core!" and break my heart, or crack me up with his Groucho-perfect rendition of "Lydia, the Tattooed Lady." We sing Tom Lehrer songs together, though I can't keep up with him on "The Elements," the periodic table set to the tune of Gilbert & Sullivan's "Major-General's Song."

Many of his friends have a theatrical flair as well. One night, coming home from his chorus concert, Joe told me about the girl in school who always dresses in Victorian garb and is pretending to be Sweeney Todd. She had asked him to be a policeman in her handmade production of the musical.

She said, "You'd be perfect as the policeman—could I slit your throat?"

His answer, he said, was "Yessss!"

"So you're not the weirdest kid in school?" I asked.

"OhGodNo," Joe said.

One evening, about a year ago, I told Joseph that I was thinking about writing a book about us. What we'd been through.

Him.

We were driving in my tiny Smart car, a two-seater that makes any conversation intimate. I had been wanting to bring up the topic for a while; a friend in the publishing world had expressed interest in a book like this one and had encouraged me to come up with a proposal. But I wasn't going to do it without Joseph's consent, and was reluctant to do it at all unless he was enthusiastic.

I laid out what such a book would say, and how it would provide a narrative thread and context in alternating chapters. That it would be about us, but about more than just us. I asked him what he thought.

"You should do it," he said.

I pointed out that the book could be uncomfortable—that I would be talking about a lot of things, including the hospital.

He bristled a bit. He doesn't like talking about those days, and he'd understood the implications the first time. With Joe, one answer is enough. "I have a dearth of caring," he said, and reminded me that he had already given his consent.

"Do it."

Over time, he grew more talkative on the subject as he became more interested in the book and its narrative, reminding me of moments from the past and helping me to fill in gaps.

"I can be gayer, if you want," he said helpfully.

"You're plenty gay enough," I replied.

CHAPTER FOURTEEN

*Study Finds Every Style of Parenting Produces
Disturbed, Miserable Adults*

—HEADLINE FROM *THE ONION*[115]

All the time Jeanne and I were struggling with the schools
and with doctors and with our own confusion, we wondered
where we could find the information that could really help us.
We looked in those racks of brochures about dealing with eating disorders and depression and everything else; where was the
brochure for us? It wasn't there.

So we wrote it.

No one could confuse this book with a step-by-step guide,
and we didn't intend it that way. Your situation, your school,
your child, all are different from ours. But we hope that reading
our story sets you on your way to writing your own guide—one
that works for you.

Our story is not over. Joseph is still very much a work in
progress—emphasis on progress. We still get a quick twinge of
nervousness when the phone rings during the day and the

school's phone number turns up on the display. And sometimes the twinge is justified. He retains the capacity to surprise us in unpleasant ways.

But more and more, we know it's getting better.

When other parents talk to me about their kids' achievements, like the one who placed out of a full year of college through AP tests, the ones who pitted Harvard against Yale to get the best scholarship package, or when they agonize publicly about whether their child will get into the elite school that will match their image of their family's abilities, I smile.

We have Joe. He is surviving adolescence. We started with three great kids, and we still have three great kids. We are confident that Joseph will go to college in a couple of years.

We're not sure where. It will be a good college, not necessarily the most prestigious one, as Lynn Field, a mental health provider who works with teenagers, wrote in a 2011 essay in the *Washington Post*. "It's clear that students in this area see applying to college as a high-stakes, make-or-break moment," she wrote. "As a mental health provider who works with teenagers, I find it heartbreaking to see the effect of this myth on the psyches of high schoolers." The important thing, she wrote, is finding the right fit.[116]

In a follow-up interview with Field, *Washington Post* blogger Janice D'Arcy asked whether there are mental health risks to getting into a prestige school that puts students under more pressure than they are equipped to deal with. Field said, "I have seen this over and over again," and told the story of a student whose family pulled strings to get her into a big-name school that had initially rejected her. Once the student got there, "She felt overwhelmed from the get-go, had a severe depressive episode, and withdrew," she said.[117]

We won't be looking for a blow-off school, but we will be wary of those high-pressure campuses whose students proudly refer to as "the place where fun goes to die." We'll be looking for a school that's really got the welcome mat out for gay kids, and can accommodate someone who is still, to use my diagnostic term, a little squirrelly.

Of all of the diagnoses people have tried to pin on Joseph, none has ever described the unique individual that is Joe. I doubt any of them ever will. We still don't understand why so many people seem to think that a child's problems have to be tagged with a diagnosis. But increasingly, we have come to learn that we aren't alone.

In January 2012, Benedict Carey wrote a startling story in the New York Times about the shifting diagnoses of autism spectrum disorder.[118] The narrowed definition that will appear in the next edition of the DSM, he wrote, will sharply cut the number of diagnoses. A study that looked at 372 high-functioning adults and children whose symptoms were used to create the current definitions found that under the new guidelines, only 45 percent of them would qualify for the proposed new definition.

That story kicked off a small flurry of essays in the Times about Asperger's syndrome. Paul Steinberg, a psychiatrist, wrote about the downside of recent decades' expanding definition. "Social disabilities are not at all trivial, but they become cheapened by the ubiquity of the Asperger's diagnosis, and they become miscast when put in the autism spectrum," he wrote, and added that "many of us clinicians have seen young adults denied job opportunities, for example in the Peace Corps, when inappropriately given a diagnosis of Asperger's syndrome instead of a social disability."

Another essayist stated "I Had Asperger's Syndrome. Briefly."[119] Benjamin Nugent, the director of the creative writing program at Southern New Hampshire University, received an Asperger's diagnosis at seventeen; by his twenties, he had overcome much of the social awkwardness that had contributed to his diagnosis. In the essay, he warned that "under the rules in place today, any nerd, any withdrawn, bookish kid, can have Asperger's syndrome." And, he wrote, "I don't want a kid with mild autism to go untreated. But I don't want a school psychologist to give a clumsy, lonely teenager a description of his mind that isn't true."

Nugent wondered whether he might have become a writer if at the tender age of twelve he had been told that he was "hardwired to find social interaction baffling."

Jeanne and I read the essays with a growing sense of wonder. After being told so many times that Joseph had Asperger's syndrome, we realized we are part of a community of people whose children may have been swept up in a psychological fad.

It was up to us to sort through it all and find out what diagnoses could usefully describe a problem Joseph had, and that we could deal with—things like the diagnosis of depression and the discovery of his handwriting problems, which turns out to be a thing called dysgraphia. The rest of them muddied the waters, and some seemed to close off opportunities. Joseph's identity has much more to do with being gay, and having to deal with a tendency toward depression, than with whatever behavioral quirk he also has. His psychological issues are a part of who he is, but not the defining part.

The things that make Joe different used to be a source of pain. Now they are part of what makes him special.

In my previous book, I spoke to kids about being short. While acknowledging that they might feel frustrated about being small—as I did growing up—I let them know there's nothing inherent in small stature that destined them for a second-class life.

I wrote about the nature of our society to medicalize every difference between us. I described efforts by pharmaceutical companies to classify being little as a condition, "idiopathic short stature," that could qualify children for treatment with expensive drugs that may or may not bring them greater height. Alice Dreger, the professor at Northwestern, called it "the American way of parenting," which she explained is "all about consumption" and "getting your kid everything you can get them."

That includes getting into the best preschool, paying for tutoring, and buying top-of-the-line sports equipment. It also, she said, means wanting to buy height, especially if the parents grew up short themselves and recalled being upset about it. Such feelings might cause the parents to discount the risks and the possible downsides of treatment, she said, and could blind them to something important: "They all made it. Many of them would be able to say, 'I emotionally benefited from this challenge.'"

That led up to the key question in that book—and perhaps, this one. Who wants to be "normal"? What does normal get you, anyway?

Dov Fox, a research fellow at Georgetown Law Center, has written that the quest to conform—to become normal—might be overrated. Reaching into the world of fiction, he noted that

Cyrano de Bergerac was a brilliant swordsman and poet who suffered because of his enormous nose. "Perhaps Cyrano would have been happier simply to have been 'normal,'" he wrote. "But we would have lost a greatness and sensitivity of soul that would have lessened all of us."[120]

Which brings us to another literary detour. Did you ever wonder why so many kids loved Harry Potter so much? In the 1990s, a gay friend at the *Washington Post* raved about the Potter series and urged other reporters to read it. I'd been reading all along, keeping up with the kids and talking with them about the adventures. But my friend's passion for the books helped me realize that the compelling idea for kids reading the series could have a special appeal to gay people. People who love Harry Potter tend to understand that it is, at its core, a celebration of the things that make us different.

Joseph loved Harry Potter, of course. And he loved *The Little Prince*, a book his older brother had no use for. Joseph really responded to the story of a lonely boy on an isolated planet who yearns for companionship. And who, as it happens, dresses in fabulous robes.

Whether they see themselves as secret wizards or little princes or Martian children, many kids feel left out of this world. It's up to us to make them feel at home. To help them feel loved. To let them be themselves. Happily.

That, by the way, is the underlying message of the work of Ritch Savin-Williams. He has, as you might imagine, been criticized for his efforts to go against the grain of research and insist that gay teens are, for the most part, doing well. When I talked with him, he said that he intends his positive message to dispel the gloom of sensationalistic reporting and to offer an alternative to the "it gets better" phenomenon.

"It's not that 'it gets better,'" he told me. "It's better *right now.*" He wants the new generation to hear a powerful message, he said: "Enjoy your life—you're just as good as anyone else. You're just as healthy as anyone else."

That's when I told him about Joe, and the pills.

He recovered nicely and responded with compassion. Yes, he said softly, some kids *are* in trouble, just as some kids do get bullied. "I want them to know they have the same rights as any kids," he said. "You have a right to demand a good, healthy life right now. *Right now.* You don't have to wait."

He asked how Joseph is doing, and I was happy to be able to tell him about moments like the purple hair episode in the locker room. He was clearly tickled to hear that a jock had stood up for Joe. "I love it!" he said.

Even if a gay youngster seems depressed, he said, "it depends on the lens you're looking through—it may be because of the very qualities we say we like in our kids." He listed some of the traits that have been attributed to so many gay kids: "Being sensitive. Being aware of others. Being sensitive to your own inner self." All of these are good qualities, but they can come at a cost. Ultimately, however, they enrich us all.

Isn't it time, he said, to "turn our attention to the good things they offer us?"

Joseph is different. He doesn't see the world as everyone else does; he is sardonic and hilarious, goofy and grand. We wouldn't have him any other way. Thinking about it brings me back to what Professor Betty Sue Flowers said to Brian:

"It's a gift."

———

In September 2011, Joseph showed me an assignment he'd turned in for a creative writing class. As one of their exercises in writing in various styles and formats, the teacher had asked for a children's book.

He wrote what he called a "ridiculously adorable kid's story" in the style of the children's author Barbara Cooney. Joe's story was about a boy who develops a crush on another boy.

He showed it to me.

I read it.

I cried.

"You might want to think about including it in your book," he suggested. He told me that the teacher showed it to her mother, who told her, "You'd better have given that boy an A, because that story made me cry."

A few days later at work, I showed it to Rich. A minute or two after I'd e-mailed it to him, he was at my desk. "That's fucking brilliant!" he said.

I hope you enjoy the last chapter. Joe wrote it.

Leo,
The Oddly
Normal Boy

by Joseph Schwartz

Leo was a young boy who was quite normal in many ways, but quite odd in other ways. Most people are, you will find.

He liked to play sports, and dance, and spin around until he was almost sick. He liked to collect flowers, and stamps, and shiny rocks, even though he usually got bored of collecting them a few days after he started.

In fact, he liked many things, and he did not think it was in any way odd that he liked boys as well.

His classmates, as you may expect, found it very odd indeed, but said nothing. He was very nice, you see, and they didn't mind that he was odd, even though his oddness confused them quite a lot.

One day he found that he liked one boy in his class, Frederick, who was very handsome (even though he was a bit mean). As he was a very logical boy, he quietly watched what his classmates did when they liked people.

He found that some of them gave their beloved flowers ...

some gave them chocolates ...

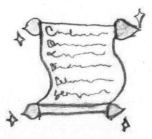

and almost all of them gave them some poetry.

So he went out and filled a paper cup with flowers he had collected ...

he spent two whole dollars on a chocolate bar from a nearby candy store ...

and he wrote some poetry himself, although even he knew that it was quite terrible.

He approached Frederick, carrying the gifts and blushing.
"I'm Leo. I— I hope you like these!"

"Don't mind the poetry, it's really bad," he mumbled while looking down at his shoes.

Frederick read the poem, and he started laughing loudly. "This is terrible! If you're trying to get me to date you, this is a pretty awful way to go about it!"

He threw the poetry on the ground and stomped on the flowers, and laughed with his friends as Leo walked away crying.

When Leo got home, he was sobbing, and he had eaten all of the chocolate, which gave him a tummy-ache on top of it all. His mother, who was very kind, noticed immediately that he was crying and had been eating chocolate, which he rarely did. "Honey, what's wrong?" she asked.

He explained to her that a boy had been very mean to him, and that he didn't want to talk about it. His mother said to him, in a very patient voice, "Are you sure?" And he started crying harder, and he explained everything.

His mother, once she heard the story, was very angry. She made it quite clear that she was angry at the other boy, and that Leo was fine.

She said, "Listen, Leo. If this boy doesn't like you, that's one thing. But he can't be mean to you just because you like him. That's just wrong."

"I want you to know that you shouldn't let it get to you, and that he's going to be punished for what he's done. Don't worry about it anymore."

"Now here's some medicine for your stomach, and in an hour or so you can eat dinner and go to bed. You've had a long, bad day and you should rest."

After he woke up the next day, he didn't want to go to school. He might see Frederick, and then he'd probably start to cry.

His mother said to him, "Leo, if you don't go to school then you'll never feel better. You've got to go on with your life, or you'll never get anything done, and if you don't get anything done, how will you become the first Emperor of the United Galaxy?"

(Becoming Emperor of the United Galaxy was Leo's greatest ambition, and any reference to it would almost always make him more enthusiastic.)

"All right, I'll go to school. I guess I have to learn to over-come hardship if I'm going to have an awesome story when I'm Emperor, right?"

So he went off to school, and inside the classroom Frederick walked up to him grumbling, with the teacher glaring at him as he walked. "Look, I'm sorry about the whole thing where I destroyed your stupid presents, okay? I shouldn't have."

Leo made sure he did not cry at all as he said, "Apology accepted. I'm not talking to you anymore." But then, as he walked to his seat, he felt a tap on his shoulder. He turned around ...

. . . and he saw another boy, blushing and carrying some flowers in a cup, a bar of chocolate, and a slightly rumpled piece of paper that looked like poetry. "I'm Francis. I— I got you these . . ."

He was a young boy who was quite normal in many ways, but quite odd in other ways. Most people are, you will find.

ACKNOWLEDGMENTS

Books are the work of many hands and many minds; this one has been shaped by everyone Jeanne and I have known. Obviously, by our parents, who made us the parents we became. And also by those teachers and therapists who were helpful, and who sustained us in difficult times.

We owe an enormous debt to the league of gay uncles, who helped guide us through Joe's adolescence. Rich Meislin, Mark Kaiserman, Jim Pearcy, and especially Brian Zabcik, who generously agreed to share his experiences and his eloquent and brave e-mails.

Mark asked me to mention that he's single. Then he said he was just joking, but I'm putting it in anyway. You never know.

Thanks to Susan Lehman, who encouraged me to come up with a proposal, and Rafe Sagalyn, my agent, who helped me shape it and offered great advice along the way. My editor at Penguin, Megan Newman, saw value in my proposal and guided me with a steady hand; Penguin also provided great talents in Melinda Ackell, Sabrina Bowers, Gigi Campo, Erica Ferguson, Beth Parker, and Elke Sigal.

Thanks, too, to the early readers: Pauline Spinrad, Jim Pearcy, Xeni Jardin, and our older kids, Elizabeth and Sam, who made important suggestions and contributions. And also to Jessica Landis, who gave Joseph the assignment of writing a children's book.

Obviously, great thanks go to Joseph, who agreed from the start that this is a book worth writing, and who talked with us about everything as I worked through the writing process. Joe read the first draft the day after I'd completed it; we sat at the dining room table as he read, with obvious emotion. His suggestions after reading that draft greatly enriched the story and rounded out the picture of a complex, wholly exceptional, and oddly normal boy.

And, of course, Jeanne. This is as much her story as it is Joe's or mine. When I told her that it looked like the proposal was going to be accepted, she simply sat down and began typing. Over the next week and a half, she hammered out 120 pages of memories, recalling details and moments that I could never have dredged up on my own. She read and reread every chapter, calling for greater clarity here, a more personal approach there—making our book better in every way. Friends raised their eyebrows when I told them that we were working on the book together; books can kill marriages. Ours has survived, so maybe we're doing something wrong. Somehow, I don't think so.

I am grateful, too, to the late Steve Jobs, whose computers come with backup software so seductively easy to use that, when my laptop died, I had an up-to-date copy of the book on an external drive and only lost a few days of editing. Whew.

Then there's the *New York Times*. You can see the newspaper from the outside as a monolithic journalism organization. You can despise it for being a tool of the Left, or for kowtowing to the Right. There are plenty of people on either side of that hate-fest. But the paper is a place whose managers know what's important when a family crisis erupts. We are expected to work as hard as we can, and each of us finds ways to work harder than we ever thought we could. When our lives go off the rails, though, the bosses show tremendous support.

Colleagues at the *Times* are an inspiration—supportive, energetic, and so damned smart. Within the broader enterprise, there is the lunch table, a daily klatch where good buddies gossip and laugh. We're like the Algonquin Round Table, but with knuckleheads. Thanks, guys: When I talked about the book, you listened.

Oddly Normal got its start because of a conversation in the newsroom. When I talked with a fellow reporter, Jacques Steinberg, about our family's experiences, he immediately urged me to share the story in print. "That book will change lives," he said.

Here's hoping.

APPENDIX

There are thousands of national and local organizations dedicated to making sure that kids who might be gay, lesbian, bisexual, or transgender grow up happy and safe. Here, a partial listing:

- PFLAG National (http://www.pflag.org/): PFLAG is an organization that unites 200,000 members and supporters in 368 chapters. As its site says, "PFLAG promotes the health and well-being of lesbian, gay, bisexual, and transgender persons, their families and friends through: support, to cope with an adverse society; education, to enlighten an ill-informed public; and advocacy, to end discrimination and to secure equal civil rights." Local chapters can be found on the site (http://www.pflag.org/findachapter).

- GSA Network (http://gsanetwork.org/): Advocates for safe schools and the creation of gay-straight alliance organizations. It offers a national directory of organizations, and tips for starting one of your own, here: http://gsanetwork.org/national-directory. The group also sponsors an activist program, the Make It Better Project (http://www.makeitbetterproject.org/) to make schools safer.

- CenterLink (http://www.lgbtcenters.org/): This network of LGBT centers offers a directory at http://www.lgbtcenters.org/Centers/find-a-center.aspx.

- Gay & Lesbian Alliance Against Defamation (http://www.glaad.org/): This group advocates for balanced media coverage of gay issues and is a sponsor of "Spirit Day," a nationwide show of support for LGBT kids and against bullying by wearing purple (http://www.glaad.org/spiritday).

- Gay, Lesbian & Straight Education Network (glsen.org): A national education organization dedicated to making schools safer and improving the climate of tolerance and acceptance in schools. Their guide to forming or improving gay-straight alliance clubs can be found at http://www.glsen.org/cgi-bin/iowa/student/library/record/2226.html. Their youth page is here: http://www.glsen.org/cgi-bin/iowa/all/student/index.html.

- It Gets Better Project (http://www.itgetsbetter.org/): Cofounded by the columnist Dan Savage, It Gets Better posts videos of encouragement for LGBT teens. The movement has gone worldwide and inspired more than 30,000 videos from everyday folks, President Barack Obama, Broadway actors, and the staff of corporations including Google and Pixar.

- The Trevor Project (http://www.thetrevorproject.org/): Dedicated to preventing suicide among lesbian, gay, bisexual, and transgender and questioning youth, this group offers a 24/7 crisis hotline (1-866-488-7386) along with online chat and community outreach, as well as education programs.
- Trans Youth Family Allies (http://imatyfa.org/): A group devoted to helping transgender youth and their families find support and deal with the prejudice and harassment. The group, based in Holland, Michigan, deals with educators, service providers and communities, and provides online support.
- Hetrick-Martin Institute: The oldest and largest nonprofit agency dedicated to help LGBT youth (between the ages of twelve and twenty-one) in New York City with services that include counseling, activities, career exploration and more; the Institute also runs the Harvey Milk High School in Manhattan.
- Fortunate Families (http://www.fortunatefamilies.org): Helps Catholic parents of LGBT kids, and families of all faiths, connect with other families and build a stronger community of support.
- Suicide Hotlines (http://www.suicidehotlines.com/): A site to find numbers for calling suicide prevention hotlines.
- StopBullying.gov (http://www.stopbullying.gov): This official government website is managed by the Department of Health & Human Services, Department of Education, and Department of Justice, with resources on bullying and schools.
- The ACLU LGBT Youth & Schools Project (http://www.aclu.org/lgbt-rights/lgbt-youth-schools): The American

Civil Liberties Union has a program to fight discrimination in schools and to encourage the formation of gay-straight alliance clubs.

- National Youth Advocacy Coalition (nyacyouth.org): A social justice organization devoted to encouraging LGBT advocacy among young people.
- Point Foundation (http://www.pointfoundation.org/index 10.html): Provides financial support and leadership training for LGBT students.
- Arcus Foundation (http://www.arcusfoundation.org): This group works to advance LGBT equality and to help conservation efforts to protect the great apes.
- Tyler Clementi Foundation: A group formed by the parents of Tyler Clementi, the Rutgers freshman who committed suicide in 2010 by jumping off the George Washington Bridge. Its goals: "To raise awareness of the issues surrounding and support organizations concerned with suicide prevention, acceptance of LGBT teens, and education against internet cyberbullying."
- Matthew Shepard Foundation (http://www.matthew shepard.org/): Created by the family of Matthew Shepard, a student at the University of Wyoming who was murdered in 1998.
- Sexuality Information and Education Council of the United States (www.siecus.org): LGBT youth information page: http://www.siecus.org/index.cfm?fuseaction=page .viewpage&pageid=605&grandparentID=477&paren tID=591#mentalhealth.
- Advocates for Youth (www.advocatesforyouth.org): A group in Washington devoted to promoting adolescent

reproductive and sexual health. Their LGBTQ pages, including information for parents: www.advocatesfor youth.org/glbtq-issues-home.

- Healthy Children (www.healthychildren.org): A site from the American Academy of Pediatrics, with a page for LGBT issues and resources: http://www.healthychildren .org/English/ages-stages/teen/dating-sex/pages/Gay-and -Lesbian-Teens.aspx.

- Soulforce (http://www.soulforce.org): A group "that works nonviolently to end the religious and political oppression of LGBTQ people," with a focus on religiously based intolerance.

- Electronic Aggression (http://www.cdc.gov/ViolencePre vention/youthviolence/electronicaggression/index.html): A site of the Centers for Disease Control and Prevention devoted to cyberbullying information and resources.

- Atticus Circle (http://www.atticuscircle.org): A group devoted to educating and mobilizing straight people to work for equal rights for LGBT folks.

ENDNOTES

1. http://www.cdc.gov/nchs/healthy_people/hp2010 /hp2010_final_review.htm

2. http://www.slate.com/articles/business/the_customer /2011/03/the_college_derby.html

3. Brown, Margaret Wise: *The Runaway Bunny*; Harper-Festival (February 27, 1991)

4. http://www.gallup.com/poll/147785/support-legal-gay -relations-hits-new-high.aspx

5. http://www.dangerousminds.net/site/john_waters_on _coming_out/

6. http://www.eric.ed.gov/ERICWebPortal/search/detailm ini.jsp?_nfpb=true&_&ERICExtSearch_SearchValue_0 =EJ597804&ERICExtSearch_SearchType_0=no &accno=EJ597804

7. http://www.hhdev.psu.edu/hdfs/faculty/pubs/Gender%
    20Atypicality%20D'Augelli%20Grossman%20Mar%
    203%20ss.pdf

8. http://books.google.com/books?id=QlqerjJTgU8C&pg
    =PA113&lpg=PA113&dq=%22the+diva+inside+unfurls
    %22+stuever&source=bl&ots=woMD1QMiru&sig
    =BGjx2VcRH99by-NleO1TclWepfg&hl=en&ei=luqOTr
    -wA8PJ0AGU7rFB&sa=X&oi=book_result&ct=result&
    resnum=1&ved=0CBoQ6AEwAA#v=onepage&q&f=false

9. http://www.metroweekly.com/feature/?ak=10

10. http://psycnet.apa.org/?&fa=main.doiLanding&doi=10
    .1037/0012-1649.31.1.43

11. http://gadgetbox.msnbc.msn.com/_news/2011/09/26
    /7968876-android-app-asks-is-my-son-gay=120S30

12. http://www.thehastingscenter.org/Publications/HCR
    /Detail.aspx?id=3124

13. http://www.nytimes.com/2012/01/29/opinion/sunday
    /childrens-add-drugs-dont-work-long-term.html?r

14. http://www.slate.com/articles/arts/books/2010/02/to
    _drug_or_not_to_drug.html

15. http://www.nytimes.com/2010/02/15/opinion/l15autism
    .html?

16. Butcher, Jim: *Princeps' Fury* (Codex Alera, Book 5) Ace
    Hardcover (November 25, 2008)

17. Heller, Joseph: *Catch-22*. Simon & Schuster; 50th
    Anniversary edition (April 5, 2011)

18. Sedaris, David: *Me Talk Pretty One Day*; Back Bay Books (June 5, 2001)

19. Høeg, Peter: *Smilla's Sense of Snow*; Picador; 20th Anniversary edition (March 27, 2012)

20. http://www.livescience.com/7177-hearing-voices-people .html

21. http://archpsyc.ama-assn.org/cgi/content/full/66/5/527

22. http://www.hcp.med.harvard.edu/ncs/index.php

23. http://www.hcp.med.harvard.edu/ncs/ftpdir/NCS-R_12 -month_Prevalence_Estimates.pdf

24. http://mentalhealth.gov/statistics/1ANYDIS_ADULT .shtml

25. http://online.wsj.com/article/SB10001424052748703959104576081920430619618.html

26. http://mentalhealth.gov/statistics/SMI_AASR .shtml

27. http://www.nyu.edu/socialwork/our.faculty/jerome.wakefield.html

28. http://www.project-syndicate.org/commentary/horwitz1 /English

29. Horwitz, Allan V. and Jerome C. Wakefield: *The Loss of Sadness*; Oxford University Press (June 18, 2007)

30. http://mentalhealth.gov/statistics/1ANYDIS_CHILD .shtml

31. http://books.google.com/books?id=L9Mj7oHEwVoC
&pg=PA713&dq=%22sociopathic+personality+distur
bance.%22+homosexuality&hl=en&ei=aBaoTsaQJub
50gGg0tmyDg&sa=X&oi=book_result&ct=result&res
num=1&ved=0CDIQ6AEwAA#v=onepage&q
=%22sociopathic%20personality%20disturbance.%22
%20homosexuality&f=false

32. http://www.lettersofnote.com/2009/10/homosexuality
-is-nothing-to-be-ashamed.html

33. http://psychology.ucdavis.edu/rainbow/html/
Herek_USCCR_Written_Testimony_050311.pdf
(footnote 5)

34. http://www.ncbi.nlm.nih.gov/pmc/articles/PMC2072932

35. http://www.stat.ucla.edu/~cochran/PDF/Estimating%
20prevalence%20of%20mental%20and%20substance%
20using%20disorders%20among%20lesbians%20
and%20gay%20men%20from%20existing%
20national%20health%20data.pdf

36. http://psychology.ucdavis.edu/rainbow/html/facts
_mental_health.html

37. http://www.cdc.gov/Features/CountingAutism

38. http://www.nichd.nih.gov/publications/pubs/upload
/introduction_autism.pdf

39. Savin-Williams, Ritch C.: *The New Gay Teenager*;
Harvard University Press (November 30, 2006)

40. Gerrold, David: *The Martian Child: A Novel About a Single Father Adopting a Son*; Tor Books; 1st edition (September 4, 2007)

41. Ibid.

42. http://ajp.psychiatryonline.org/article.aspx?articleid=174675

43. http://query.nytimes.com/gst/fullpage.html?res=9C03E6DC1E30F935A35755C0A9619C8B63&scp=1

44. http://www.funnyordie.com/videos/c0cf508ff8/prop-8-the-musical-starring-jack-black-john-c-reilly-and-many-more-from-fod-team-jack-black-craig-robinson-john-c-reilly-and-rashida-jones

45. http://www.nj.com/news/index.ssf/2010/09/tyler_clementis_death_is_mourn.html

46. http://gawker.com/5651659/is-this-webcam-spying-victim-tyler-clementis-last-call-for-help

47. http://www.nytimes.com/2010/09/30/nyregion/30suicide.html?

48. http://137.187.25.243/library/mentalhealth/chapter3/sec5.html

49. http://www.cdc.gov/ViolencePrevention/pdf/Suicide_DataSheet-a.pdf

50. http://www.eurekalert.org/pub_releases/2011-04/cums-sls041311.php

51.   http://www.ncbi.nlm.nih.gov/pmc/articles
      /PMC1446760

52.   http://www.psychologytoday.com/blog/the-sexual
      -continuum/201012/new-research-mental-health-and
      -suicide-attempts-in-lesbian-gay-bise

53.   http://www.annenbergpublicpolicycenter.org/ProjectDe
      tails.aspx?myId=28

54.   http://www.glsen.org/binary-data/GLSEN_ATTACH
      MENTS/file/000/001/1675-2.pdf

55.   http://www.campuspride.org/Campus%20Pride%
      202010%20LGBT%20Report%20Summary.pdf

56.   http://www.ncbi.nlm.nih.gov/pubmed/17057162

57.   http://journals.lww.com/jrnldbp/Abstract/2007/04000
      /Psychometric_Properties_of_the_Peer_Interactions.8.aspx

58.   Ryan C, Huebner D, Diaz RM, Sanchez J. "Family
      rejection as a predictor of negative health outcomes in
      white and Latino lesbian, gay, and bisexual young adults,"
      Pediatrics 123 (2009): 346–352.

59.   http://familyproject.sfsu.edu/overview

60.   http://www.eurekalert.org/pub_releases/2011-04/cums
      -sls041311.php

61.   http://www.splcenter.org/get-informed/news/splc-sues
      -minnesota-school-district-to-protect-lgbt-students-from
      -harassment-hosti

62. http://www.nytimes.com/2011/09/13/us/13bullysidebar.html

63. http://motherjones.com/politics/2011/07/michele
     -bachmann-teen-suicide

64. http://minnesota.publicradio.org/display/web/2011/07/21
     /lawsuit-filed-in-anoka-hennepin-suit

65. http://www.bachmanncounseling.com

66. http://www.advocate.com/Politics/Commentary/In_His
     _Own_Words__How_I_Went_Undercover_at_Bach
     mann_s_Clinic

67. http://www.huffingtonpost.com/2011/12/16/marcus-
     bachmann-ex-gay-therapy-bill-activist-_n_1153899
     .html

68. http://www.citypages.com/content/printVersion/17190

69. http://minnesotaindependent.com/71696/minnesota
     -family-council-pushes-back-in-anoka-hennepin-anti-gay
     -bullying-controversy

70. http://www.startribune.com/local/north/104187928
     .html?page=1&c=y

71. http://www.anoka.k12.mn.us/education/page/download
     .php?fileinfo=NjA0LjQwX1Jlc3BlY3RmdWxfTGVhc
     m5pbmdfRW52aXJvbm1lbnRfLV9DdXJyaWN1bHVtX
     1BvbGljeS5wZGY6Ojovd3d3Ni9zY2hvb2x
     zL21uL2Fub2thL2ltYWdlcy9kb2NtZ3IvMTUwNDl
     maWxlMTE3NTA0LnBkZg==

72. http://www.nytimes.com/2012/03/07/education/minne
     sota-district-reaches-pact-on-antigay-bullying.html?scp
     =1&sq=anoka&st=cse

73. http://www.startribune.com/local/north/141427303
     .html?page=all&prepage=1&c=y#continue

74. http://swampland.time.com/2011/11/04/why-does
     -michigans-anti-bullying-bill-protect-religious
     -tormenters/#ixzz1glCWOklb

75. http://onfaith.washingtonpost.com/onfaith/panelists
     /debra_w_haffner/2010/10/an_open_letter_to_religious
     _leaders_on_gay_youth_suicides_its_time_to_act_out
     _loud.html

76. http://www.nytimes.com/2007/03/28/us/28risk.html

77. http://library-resources.cqu.edu.au/JFS/PDF/vol_40/iss
     _4/JFS404950574.pdf

78. http://childstudycenter.yale.edu/autism/information/pdd
     nos.aspx

79. http://www.usatoday.com/life/television/2002
     /2002-03-11-coming-out-timeline.htm

80. Russo, Vito: *The Celluloid Closet*; Harper & Row
     (September 20, 1987)

81. http://today.msnbc.msn.com/id/36739351/ns/today
     -books/t/archie-comics-unveils-gay-character

82. http://today.msnbc.msn.com/id/44577649/ns/today
     -books/t/gay-characters-take-center-stage-comic-books
     /#.TvJ29pj5Aws

83. http://news.bbc.co.uk/2/hi/276677.stm

84. http://www.foxnews.com/us/2011/09/14/archie-comics
     -confirms-gay-marriage-storyline-will-anyone-
     object/#ixzz1Y59Ptj4P

85. http://townhall.com/columnists/kevinmccullough/2011
     /11/06/glees_gay_garden_goes_too_far

86. http://www.gallup.com/poll/118931/Knowing-Someone
     -Gay-Lesbian-Affects-Views-Gay-Issues.aspx

87. http://www.nytimes.com/2004/02/07/arts/love-that-dare
     -not-squeak-its-name.html

88. http://www.emperor-penguin.com/gay-penguins
     .html

89. http://shelf-life.ew.com/2011/04/12/ala-most-frequently
     -challenged-books-201

90. http://www.apa.org/about/offices/ogc/amicus/lawrence
     .pdf

91. http://www.nytimes.com/2007/01/25/science/25sheep
     .html?

92. http://andrewsullivan.thedailybeast.com/2007/01/more
     _on_gay_she.html

93. http://www.law.cornell.edu/supct/html/02-102.ZS.html

94. http://www.law.cornell.edu/supct/html/94-1039.ZO
     .html

95. http://documents.nytimes.com/us-district-court-decision
     -perry-v-schwarzenegger?ref=us

96. http://www.ncsl.org/default.aspx?tabid=16430

97. http://www.nytimes.com/2009/05/28/us/28marriage
.html?pagewanted=all

98. http://www.nytimes.com/2009/08/19/us/19olson.html
?pagewanted=all

99. http://www.nytimes.com/2010/09/22/us/22legal.html?s

100. http://www.nytimes.com/2007/09/27/science/27expelled
.html?

101. http://www.nytimes.com/2010/08/06/us/06walker.html?

102. http://www.nytimes.com/2007/05/27/fashion/weddings
/27spyer.html

103. http://www.nytimes.com/2010/11/09/us/09marriage
.html?

104. http://www.nytimes.com/2010/07/09/us/09marriage
.html

105. http://www.justice.gov/opa/pr/2011/February/11-ag-223
.html

106. http://www.nytimes.com/2011/02/24/us/24marriage
.html?

107. http://www.nytimes.com/2010/09/10/us/10gays.html

108. http://www.nytimes.com/2010/09/22/us/22legal.html?
scp=5

109. http://www.nytimes.com/2012/05/10/us/politics/obama
-says-same-sex-marriage-should-be-legal.html?

110. http://www.ca9.uscourts.gov/datastore/general/2012/02
/07/1016696com.pdf

111. http://www.nytimes.com/2007/01/07/education/edlife
/07notebook.html?scp=1&sq=PONCHO%20BEARER
&st=cse

112. http://www.urbandictionary.com/define.php?term=Gay
%20As%20Christmas

113. http://www.nytimes.com/2011/08/31/nyregion
/bullying-law-puts-new-jersey-schools-on-spot.html?
pagewanted=all

114. http://ideas.time.com/2011/09/06/why-new-jerseys
-antibullying-law-should-be-a-model-for-other
-states/#ixzz1hHZHgKXw

115. http://www.theonion.com/articles/study-finds-every
-style-of-parenting-produces-dist,26452

116. http://www.washingtonpost.com/opinions/setting-our
-sights-on-a-good-enough-college/2011/12/16/gIQAyC
K8yO_story.html

117. http://www.washingtonpost.com/blogs/on-parenting
/post/is-a-good-enough-college-the-best-college/2011/12
/18/gIQANNiN3O_blog.html

118. http://www.nytimes.com/2012/01/20/health/research
      /new-autism-definition-would-exclude-many-study
      -suggests.html?

119. http://www.nytimes.com/2012/02/01/opinion/i-had
      -asperger-syndrome-briefly.html?ref=opinion

120. http://works.bepress.com/dov_fox/11